How to Talk to a Man and Feel Heard

9 Mistakes Women Need To Avoid

Improve couples communication skills, reduce conflict, repair your marriage, and create a healthy relationship.

Sue Shepard, MFT

Anecdotes and stories presented in the book are composites of actual people. Names and other details have been changed to protect identities.

Copyright © 2022 Sue Shepard, MFT
Published in the United States of America, 2022

All rights reserved. No portion of this book may be reproduced, stored in a retrieval system, or transmitted in any form or by any means – electronic, mechanical, photocopy, recording, or any other – except for brief quotations in a book review, without the prior written permission of the author or publisher. For more information, contact sueshepard@therapybysue.com

First edition, 2022

ISBN 979-8-9857761-1-9 (paperback)
ISBN 979-8-9857761-3-3 (ebook)
ISBN 979-8-9857761-8-8 (hardback)

Cover design by Brandi Doane McCann at:
   www.ebook-coverdesigns.com
Interior book design by Saqib Arshad at:
   www.fiverr.com/saqib_arshad
Author photo by Lorin Backe at:
   www.lorinbackephotography.com

Contents

INTRODUCTION 1

MISTAKE #1 7
   A Mistake That Leads to Disillusionment & Disappointment

MISTAKE #2 31
   A Mistake That Leads to Him Feeling Incompetent

MISTAKE #3 55
   A Mistake That Leads to False Assumptions

MISTAKE #4 69
   A Mistake That Leads to Competitiveness

MISTAKE #5 79
   A Mistake That Leads to Him Shutting Down

MISTAKE #6 95
   A Mistake That Leads to Unsuccessful Conversations

MISTAKE #7 111
   A Mistake That Leads to Defensiveness

MISTAKE #8 131
   A Mistake That Leads to Your Needs Not Being Met

MISTAKE #9 153
   A Mistake That Leads to Resentment
FINAL WORDS 175
ABOUT THE AUTHOR 179
REFERENCES 181

Introduction

If this book title attracted your attention, then it's likely that you are not feeling heard in your current relationship, or you have experienced this in past relationships.

Unfortunately, you are not alone. The most common complaint that women in relationships have is: I don't feel heard.[1] In addition to wanting to be heard, women also want to be understood. However, you cannot begin to be understood until you learn to speak in a manner where what you say is what he hears.

This book is relevant for women of all ages who are just starting a relationship or have been married for years. It will also benefit single and single-again women in the dating world. By learning to avoid the mistakes described in this book, you will gain insight that will enable you to communicate in a way that allows you to be heard and understood.

Communication is challenging in any relationship because no two people communicate identically. As a result, you could do or say things in your relationship that he might not perceive in the manner you intended. I share the mistakes women need to avoid and suggest little things you can do differently to favorably impact your current or future relationships and increase the likelihood of being heard.

I am not asking you to make sizable changes that will cause you to give up being fully yourself. That is absolutely not healthy for you or your relationship. I regard these more as *shifts* in your relationship, similar to those you make when traveling to a foreign country. If you are like most travelers, as you prepare for travel outside of the county, you try to learn about the differences in their language, customs, and culture. Equipped with this knowledge, you hold on to who you are as you travel, but you may avoid certain words or gestures when you discover that locals could interpret them as offensive in their country.

I have been doing couples counseling for more than twenty years. I ask each couple what they hope to achieve while in therapy, and hands down, the number one response is "better communication." They understand that if their communication improves, the rest of the problems/challenges/issues in their relationship will also change for the better.

Even though I am writing this book to all women, please realize that everything I present will not apply to *all* women. I will be sharing generalizations that will help most women, but it would be impossible to help all women because you each have unique characteristics. Inevitably, there will be exceptions. I hope you will read with eyes looking for what is most important to *you* and *your* situation and let anything that does not pertain to you remain on the page, knowing that another reader may find something that applies to them where you might not.

A special note to you if you are the more rational, thinking type and your guy is the emotional, feeling person in the relationship. If that sounds like you, you'll benefit most by staying open and ignoring what gender is assigned to the traits mentioned in this book. Instead, look for what characteristics you resonate most with and apply that information to whichever one of you is more appropriate.

I would also like to mention that I am writing this assuming that the man you are trying to communicate with is a relatively decent guy. He may not be perfect, but he is essentially a good man. On the other hand, suppose you are trying to be heard by an abusive man or a man diagnosed with a mental illness, alcoholism, substance abuse, or a personality disorder. In that case, you may need more help than this book can offer and most likely could benefit from some personalized, professional therapy.

There is a possibility that you might become frustrated as you read this because it feels like I am putting all the responsibility on you. For that reason, I want to assure you that I am aware that both of you share responsibility for the communication difficulties you are experiencing in your relationship. If I had the privilege of seeing you for couple's counseling in my private practice, I would encourage each of you to take ownership of your part of the problem and advise both of you to make changes.

Since you are the one reading (or listening) to this book, not your partner, I am addressing my comments to the aspects of your communication that you have the power to change. It is usually the dissatisfied partner who is motivated to change. You took the time to find a book to improve your communication, so I am concentrating all my attention on you and what you can do differently to increase your ability to feel heard. I am not blaming you for the challenges you are experiencing. Instead, I am sharing patterns I have seen with my clients to help you avoid mistakes as you try a different approach. One way to ensure relationship failure is to wait for the other person to change. I applaud you for taking action on your behalf.

Just because you have been talking since you were little doesn't automatically guarantee that you are skilled in doing it effectively, especially with the man in your life. The good news is that because communication is a skill, it's never too late to learn how to do it with greater success. However, before you can enhance your communication abilities, you must first determine where refinement is needed.

Take your time reading through the chapters and learning about each mistake. Next, take an honest look at your conversations and arguments with your partner. See if any of these mistakes play a role in why you often feel unheard. Then, with new insight and understanding into how his conversational style differs from yours, you can make simple changes that will have a noticeable effect on your ability to communicate more effectively. Subsequently, the new way you talk to him will reduce his defenses and create more opportunities for you to feel heard.

Mistake #1

A Mistake That Leads to Disillusionment & Disappointment

It is a mistake to liken closeness to sameness. You may not even know how many expectations you have for the man you love to feel, think, behave, or see the world the same way you do. Likewise, it is a mistake to presume that his experience is the same as yours and that words and behaviors mean the same to him as they do to you.

Reframing Male-female Conversation as Cross-cultural Communication

Deborah Tannen, a Georgetown University linguistics professor, has done substantial research on the differences in conversation style related to gender. Tannen's information benefits couples because it looks at the male-female conversation as a cross-cultural communication rather than deeming either party as *not enough of this* or *too much of that*. We would never go into another culture and argue that the native speakers are wrong because they do not converse as we do. By looking at male-female conversation from a cross-cultural point of view, we avoid judging who is right or wrong. Instead, the focus becomes learning and recognizing the differences between how men and women communicate to seek mutual respect and understanding.

According to Tannen:

> Male-female conversation is cross-cultural communication. Culture is simply a network of habits and patterns gleaned from past experience, and women and men have different past experiences. From the time they're born, they're treated differently, talked to differently, and talk differently as a result. Boys and girls grow up in different worlds, even if they grow up in the same house. And as adults, they travel in different worlds, reinforcing patterns established in childhood. These cultural differences include different expectations about the role of talk in relationships and how it fulfills that role.[2(p125)]

What if You Adopted the Premise That He Grew up in a Foreign Country?

Anyone who enjoys traveling to foreign countries understands that part of the allure of traveling is meeting new people and experiencing a culture unlike your own. You would never expect the locals there to be exactly like you. In preparation for your trip, there are several things you may do. For example, you may read a book on your chosen country or destination and browse through travel blogs on the internet. You might take the time to learn some basic ways to communicate if they speak a different language. Additionally, you might reach out to someone you know who has traveled there previously so they can share insight about the culture from a foreigner's point of view and advise you on what to anticipate and how to conduct yourself while there.

What if you were to adopt the premise that your guy grew up in a foreign country and that this book can be used as a guide to avoid mistakes typically made when conversing with someone raised in this unfamiliar territory? Consider me a fellow traveler that has spent much time with locals from this foreign territory. Recall a time when you were excited to learn about another culture and embrace that enthusiasm now as you open yourself up to learn and explore some differences in the way men and women communicate.

A Truth You Must Embrace

In my private practice, I hear women express these complaints often:

- He doesn't listen
- He won't talk
- He never shares his feelings

And I hear men make these complaints frequently:

- She's too emotional
- She talks too much
- She's too sensitive

What is interesting if you look at these two lists carefully is that each one is hoping for the same thing: Why can't they be more like me?

As a result, men and women can become immovable by the judgment of each side believing their way is better. There will always be disillusionment and disappointment if you hope he will respond to you more like the women in your life. Channel this hope into something you can attain. You can only begin to move away from this unrealistic hope by embracing the truth: *he is not you*. By the sheer fact that he is a man, and you are not, he will experience what you say differently and respond to you differently.

In order to communicate more effectively, it is essential that you grasp how dissimilarly you two see and experience things. To speak in a manner that he can hear you will require that you understand where he is coming from. You may not understand his logic or point of view, but it's vital that you still view it as valid and on the same level as yours.[3]

I will share the differences that I repeatedly see with couples in my office, which lead to unnecessary misunderstandings and heartache in relationships. Of course, not all men and women are the same, so I do not mean to imply that everything fits nicely into hard-and-fast categories. However, I have seen these patterns play out often enough with the couples I've counseled over the past two decades that it's inevitable that you'll find something in this chapter that will resonate with you.

Men and Women Talk and Listen for Different Reasons

Most women see communication as a way to develop a bond with the listener to bring them closer together. They feel the essential ingredient of communication is building relationship. So they often engage in conversation simply to connect rather than to dispense any pertinent information.

On the other hand, men primarily adhere to the belief that the single purpose of communication is to convey information to another person. Therefore, a man will typically not speak unless he has something useful to say. That's because he believes that if someone engages in a conversation, they should offer new, instructive, helpful and logical information.[4]

Can you see why the majority of couples coming in to see me for relationship therapy identify communication as their primary area of conflict? From the first word that leaves your mouth, you two are already at odds because each of you sees the purpose of communication so differently. When you are sharing your feelings in hopes of connecting, he may find it quite difficult to comprehend such an encounter and become downright perplexed and frustrated as a result. The goal is to be more empathic towards your partner as you begin to understand how differently each of you experiences a verbal exchange.

Even the Way You Each Stand While Talking Differs

Have you ever felt irritated when talking to your guy, and he won't face you and look you in the eye? Does it make you feel like he's not listening? When you were a little girl, it was typical to interact with other girls by facing each other, and eye contact is something you probably became comfortable with at an early age. Therefore, it makes sense that you would interpret his body language as his lack of interest in what you are saying and have a hard time believing he is listening when he won't look at you.

Unfortunately, you would be wrong in most cases because men customarily talk to each other side by side rather than face to face. When men converse, they tend to look off into the distance rather than make direct eye contact. Within their male culture, this is perfectly acceptable, and that is why he may not understand when you are offended by it. By comprehending that the way he stands and where he looks is his conversational style, you can stop seeing it as an indication of whether he is listening or not. Removing your judgment allows him to talk in a manner that he is comfortable with. Over time, he may become more relaxed and secure in your presence and attempt more face time.

In the following case, that is precisely the outcome that transpired. A client shared her frustration about her boyfriend, who she had been dating for only a few months. She said that every time she started to talk about something important, he would close his eyes and put his hands over his face. It made her so angry that she usually stormed off and did not attempt to share with him.

I questioned whether she had ever asked him why he did that? She said she hadn't asked because she assumed he was signaling that he didn't want to talk. So I encouraged her to ask him directly why he did that and let me know what he said.

When my client returned for her next session, she was eager to reveal what she had found out. She discovered her boyfriend was closing his eyes and covering his face to block out all distractions so he could give her his full attention. She told him how she had misinterpreted his actions, and it opened up a meaningful conversation. Once she understood his behavior was him attempting to listen intently, she started sharing freely instead of shutting down. Over time, he willingly started giving her more eye contact because even though it was somewhat uncomfortable for him, he knew it meant a lot to her.

This case illustrates why it is crucial to understand how he differs from you. Without my client seeking to understand what her boyfriend's actions meant, that relationship would not have lasted. Instead, she would have continued to be hurt by what she perceived as his unwillingness to listen to her, and it would have been only a matter of time before she walked away.

Some Men Demonstrate They Are Listening Differently Than Women

The following information is not universal to all men. I only include it because it may apply to your situation, and if it does, I would be remiss in not covering it.

When you are sharing with your guy, does he remain quiet? Does his lack of verbal input make you feel like he is not listening? When you accuse him of not listening, does he swear he is? If so, what could be occurring is that his way of listening is different than yours.

It's understandable why you may regard his silence as evidence of him not listening. You probably came to that conclusion because you are used to your female friends giving you little listening signals like "mmhmm," "uh-huh," and "yeah" while you are talking. He may think he is respectfully listening to you by staying silent because he has acquired a male conversational style that "expects a listener to be quietly attentive."[5(p142)] If he embraces that belief, his silence does not indicate that he is not listening, and you may be misinterpreting his behavior.

Truthfully, only he knows whether he is listening or not. But if he swears he is, then it is worth your effort to check with him and understand whether his listening style differs from yours so you can better understand why he remains quiet. It would be a shame to go on feeling he was not listening when he was just listening quietly.

Why He Offers You a Solution When You Just Want His Support

If you are like most women, you like to talk through your problems because as you verbally break down the issues, you can make sense of the situation and find solutions. If you were talking to another woman, she would listen intently, giving you plenty of space to express your feelings and offer support and empathy as needed.

Conversely, when your guy listens to you, he usually focuses on gathering information to solve your problem. When he hears you express your problematic situation, he most likely thinks it is an invitation to provide you with a solution. That's because most men only verbalize their concerns if they cannot figure out a solution independently. Only then do they seek additional expertise to solve the problem. Honestly, it may be a foreign concept to him that you are not seeking a solution and instead only desire emotional support.

Undoubtedly, from time to time, you have been on the receiving end of him offering you a solution when all you wanted was for him to listen to you and provide support. That's because he probably does not understand that as you express yourself, you can explore the situation from multiple viewpoints and frequently discover the solution on your own. Furthermore, since he does his problem-solving in silence, your behavior may be strange to him and hard to understand.

The social construct he follows says: solve your problems by yourself and only speak up to pursue expert advice. He operates entirely within the conversational rules taught to him by other males when he offers you a solution. He is sincerely providing you with what he believes you want. He legitimately is not trying to minimize your concerns, even though his behavior may inadvertently come across as him lacking empathy.

It is usually at the point in the conversation when you expect to receive support and instead receive a solution, that miscommunication commences and conflict quickly erupts. If you have the wrong idea of where he is coming from, you will judge him harshly for this behavior and may assign unkind labels when he offers an unwelcomed solution. He is not trying to be insensitive or uncaring – he is simply responding like a man.

This difference promises to derail your conversations and inflict hurt on one another if you don't realize that he is coming from a place of caring when he offers you a solution you didn't ask for.

Men and Women Process Stress Differently

The differences in how and when you choose to talk will show up when either one of you is stressed. Not understanding this contrast will result in needless conflict and unnecessary pain in your relationship. That's why it is essential to grasp just how differently you each behave when stressed, or it will lead to judgment and hurt feelings.

See what a wide gap exists between how men and women process their stress:

- When a woman is bothered by something that has occurred during the day, she gains the most relief from talking it through in great detail. She can go from feeling overwhelmed to feeling better through the activity of verbally processing the problem. Since most women benefit from this method, they are comfortable openly sharing their vulnerable feelings and do not consider it a burden to listen to a friend. In addition, they are not worried about being judged by other women for their weaknesses. A woman feels good when she can openly express feelings and problems to a trusted person.

- In contrast, when a man is troubled by something that went wrong during the day, he often does not want to talk about it. Instead, he prefers to withdraw and be alone while he focuses on solving his problem. If he cannot readily solve his dilemma, he may choose to do something mindless like watching TV or scrolling through the news feed on his phone. These activities allow him to detach from his troubles and experience some relief until he can seek a resolution. A man feels good when he finds the solution to his problem on his own.

Let me show you how this difference could be impeding your ability to be heard.

The man in your life may not be able to make sense of your need to talk through your problems. Instead, he might covertly (or overtly) judge you for talking too much and start to disconnect from listening to you. Since your behavior is foreign to him, he could easily deem your chatter unnecessary and feel very justified in tuning you out. From his frame of reference, this is a rational conclusion. I am not condoning his behavior because I realize how hurtful it is to you. At the same time, I hope you can see that his actions are based solely on his misunderstanding of your differences and are not indicative of how much he cares for you.

Say you are sharing about another bad day you've had at work. While you are sharing details about your ongoing struggles, he quickly responds, "If you're so miserable there, why don't you just quit?" Now your feelings are hurt because it feels like he shut you down and doesn't care about you or your problems. Take another look at this objectively from his point of view. He thought he was showing his concern by voicing a way you could put an end to your misery.

Yes, it's probably also true that he was trying to shut you up. He may feel this way as a result of him not comprehending that as you're verbalizing your frustrations of the day, you are also working through them. Within his cultural norm, he's been conditioned to work through his problems in silence and only vocalize them when he's soliciting a solution. So, he can't fathom why you would continue to talk about a problem when you aren't willing to do something about it. To him, it sounds like endless complaints without any action.

You can't expect him to fully comprehend who you are and what you want for biological and cultural reasons.[6] He will need your help to gain an understanding of why you just want him to listen to you without interrupting with solutions. So your best chance at harmony in your relationship is for you to grasp this difference and learn to take it in stride. When you do that without reacting, then you can gently guide him towards what you want or need.

Use the example above where you are sharing and need his support, and instead, he provides you with a solution. If you were to warmly respond, "I can feel how much you care about me when you offer me a solution. However, that's not what I am looking for at this time. What would really make me happy right now is just to have your support. I feel most supported by you when you assure me everything is going to be okay and just let me share my feelings without interruption."

By responding in this manner, you have accepted that his conversational style of providing solutions is just what he knows how to do best, and you recognize that he does it from a place of caring. By not reacting negatively to the unwanted solution and positively acknowledging him, he will hear you when you share what he can do to make you happy.

Silence Is as Fundamental to Him as Talking Is to You

If you are like most women, you prefer words over silence. Consequently, it may be challenging for you to understand why he becomes silent. Look at these examples and how they contrast[1]:

> While he may choose to be silent when he has a problem and wants to have time to think it through on his own to formulate a solution,
>
> IN CONTRAST: She chooses to talk and think out loud. While talking, she can explore the problem from all sides and discover what her next step will or will not be.
>
> ***
>
> While he may choose to be silent when he gets stressed and is feeling upset or angry so he can calm down and regain control before speaking,

IN CONTRAST: She chooses to talk when she is upset because it helps her get over it. Talking allows her to calm down and be more at peace.

***

While he may choose to be silent and disconnect when he fears too much intimacy has caused him to lose himself,

IN CONTRAST: She talks to cultivate intimacy. When she is vulnerable and shares her inner self, she is most connected to her loving self.

Is it any wonder why you may misinterpret his silence? Reframing his silence as a cultural difference will feel less personal and allow you to tolerate it. I hope that once you understand that his silence is just as much a part of him as talking is a part of you, you will not take it personally when he chooses silence and be more at peace with it.

Once you realize how vital silence is to his well-being, hopefully, you can become more supportive while he disconnects and is quiet. You will also benefit because he will reconnect with you sooner if he feels supported while taking time out from talking.

I have provided a handful of ways you can support him when he becomes silent and pulls away:

- Show approval of his need for silence by being okay with it
- Show him you are okay with his silence by not looking like a lost puppy when he pulls away
- Show you believe in him by not worrying about him or feeling sorry for him (or yourself)
- Show you trust he will find his own solution by not offering him any solutions
- Show you are confident he will reconnect when he is ready by not trying to facilitate conversation before he initiates it

He will find it much easier to engage again when he doesn't think he will be in trouble for his need for silence. At the same time, your need to talk is equally as important. So please reach out to a girlfriend, sister, or mom to satisfy your longing for connection.

Words May Not Have the Same Meaning to Each of You

Miscommunication may be responsible for igniting a lot of friction when you think you are on the same page and later discover that you both had completely different ideas of what you communicated.

For example, say you are having lots of family and friends over for the holidays. You turn to your husband and say, "We've got lots of people coming over today, and I'm really going to need your help." He replies, "I'm willing to help with anything you need." You leave the conversation feeling good and that you're in agreement.

Then as the day progresses, you start to get madder and madder because he isn't being helpful at all. You expected that he would take the initiative to seek you out and ask how he could assist you. Unfortunately, his expectation was quite the opposite. He thought you would reach out to him when you needed help.

So even though it seemed you were on the same page about you needing help and him agreeing to help you, the miscommunication occurred because you two had different assumptions of what *help* meant. He was more than willing to help. He just didn't understand what that looked like to you. It is a mistake to assume that the words you use hold the same meaning to him. That's why it is essential to elaborate on how he can specifically help you so he knows what you expect of him and you can trust your needs will be met.

Here is another scenario where the different meanings of words lead to miscommunication and the result was a ruined party. It was the first holiday that Ashley and Alex were dating. Ashley planned to accompany Alex to a Christmas party with lots of his extended family that she had never met. Ashley was somewhat shy and feeling rather anxious about being in this significant social situation. On their way over to the party, Ashley expressed how she was feeling and asked him not to leave her alone. Alex readily agreed, and Ashley felt comforted by his support.

Later that evening, while talkative Aunt Mable was rattling on about her physical problems, Alex walked away from the conversation. Ashley thought he would be back momentarily, but he didn't return. By the time she was able to break free from Aunt Mable's endless conversation, Ashley was furious with her boyfriend. She ended up giving him the silent treatment for the remainder of the party, and then a huge fight broke out on the drive home.

Ashley's anger erupted when Alex claimed he didn't know what he did wrong. "You promised not to leave me alone!" she cried. "I didn't," he retorted. "You left me with Aunt Mable!" Alex replied, "I know - I made sure you were never alone." Their different meaning of "don't leave me alone" was responsible for a miserable evening.

When Ashley asked Alex not to leave her alone, her expectation was for him to remain by her side the entire evening. Unfortunately, Alex took the meaning of "don't leave me alone" literally and made sure Ashley was never standing by herself. Alex felt he had lived up to her expectations without understanding that she meant something completely different.

To avoid entering into a situation like Ashley and Alex, please don't assume the words you use have identical meanings to your guy. Instead, take the time to explain what you mean and ask him what he means. Adding this simple step can prevent countless misunderstandings and heartache.

Hit Pause and Seek Clarification

When your husband or boyfriend says something that upsets you or he reacts poorly to something you said for no good reason, hit pause before you launch into an argument. Remember that you two may be bumping up against cultural communication differences, and what was said may not mean the same thing to both of you. It will save you from engaging in an unnecessary fight if you take a moment to check in with him.

If you became upset with something he said, ask:

> You just said (repeat what he said). I took that to mean (explain how you interpreted it). Is that what you meant?

If he reacted poorly to something you said and it seems like his reaction is unexpected or extreme, ask:

> I just said (repeat what you said). Please explain what that meant to you because I think it may not have been what I was trying to say, and I would like to clarify so there are no misunderstandings.

Every time the conversation starts to go wrong, and you take the time to pause and seek clarification, you give him the benefit of the doubt by recognizing that communication style differences may be in play. Doing so will save both of you a lot of heartache. As a result, not only will your relationship start to flourish, but you are also tremendously improving your chances of being heard.

Acceptance Creates Connection – Tolerance Creates Separation

His differences are just that – they are different. They are not bad or wrong. Deciding they are incorrect or seeing them as inferior is a judgment.

It is not the differences that separate you, but rather your judgments of those differences. Judgment creates a barrier between you two and restricts your ability to connect with him. To restore connection and lovingly move towards him requires your acceptance. Acceptance involves you respecting and embracing his differences and not just tolerating them.

It is crucial that you understand how accepting and tolerating are not the same thing, specifically when it pertains to the health of your relationship. From the outside, both tolerating and accepting behavior can appear to be the same.[7] However, it is the feelings you hold onto inside that distinguish one from the other.

Remaining in a state of tolerance will harm your relationship because your disapproval will continually manifest as one or more of the feelings listed below:

- Anger
- Frustration
- Resentment
- Dissatisfaction
- Disgust
- Unhappiness
- Irritation
- Annoyance
- Disrespect
- Criticism
- Sarcasm
- Judgment

If you judge his differences, you have not entirely accepted them and are still tolerating them. When your state of mind is one of tolerance rather than acceptance, you:

- Focus on his annoying characteristics
- Frequently have negative thoughts about him
- Get into arguments about things about him that are unlikely to change
- Feel never-ending tension in the relationship

- React to him in an emotionally-charged manner
- Feel exhausted after spending much time together

Tolerating is not a strategy for the long haul because it is a heavy burden to carry and will wear you both down over time. However, when you accept his differences, your struggle lessens because you no longer see the differences as all-consuming. Instead, you start to approach them as minor aspects of who he is and realize that he has so much more to offer. Acceptance allows you to embrace the differences as a necessary part of what makes him who he is.

Once you have moved from tolerance to acceptance, you are:

- Not consumed with negativity
- Free from the desire to change him
- Able to love and appreciate him as he is
- Able to enjoy your relationship despite the disparity
- Able to react in a more neutral manner that is without judgment

If you want to build your relationship to last, you'll need to expect, respect, and accept his differences. When you try to hold on to the illusion of sameness and reality starts to reveal itself, you will inevitably blame him for each departure from the fantasy you have created. For that reason, you need to let go of any wishful thinking that longs for you both to be fully in sync. Instead of idealizing a relationship based on the false belief that sameness equates to closeness, you can achieve a genuine connection based on the reality of what you each uniquely have to offer.

Lasting, healthy relationships are ones where the differences are not denied or minimized. Instead, the lack of likeness is honored and valued.[8] Through acceptance, you can move towards integrating your differences into a harmonious relationship where you both are fully seen and heard.

Mistake #1 – Top Takeaway Tips

- ♥ Relinquish the illusion of sameness
- ♥ Hit pause & seek clarification
- ♥ Expect, respect & accept the differences

Mistake #2

A Mistake That Leads to Him Feeling Incompetent

It is a mistake to offer unsolicited advice to a man. To understand why unwelcomed advice is so damaging to your relationship, it is essential to first become aware of a man's hidden vulnerability.

Without Understanding, Harmful Mistakes Happen

I had this dialogue with a guy I was dating a decade before I understood how men and women communicate differently. This interaction highlights how both a man and a woman can be in the same conversation, yet have a vastly different experience.

I was used to hanging out with my girlfriends, so I was completely unaware of how different my boyfriend would interpret my words. One of my favorite walking buddies is my friend Carol. What I love about Carol is her enormous imagination and creativity. When we would go on a walk, I could make a simple statement, like "I never see lights on in that house," and in a blink of an eye, Carol would respond, "Oh, it is a sorrowful story. His wife died two years ago. He feels so sad without her in the house that he can't bring himself to light up the house since she is gone." Bam, she was off on a tale about this house and its residents, and I got to ask questions about their life the entire walk while Carol would seamlessly provide me detailed answers that never ceased to amaze me. Even though I knew she was making it up, she made it feel so real. To this day, I cannot pass that house without feeling a little sad for the imaginary husband.

With that in mind, I was in a new relationship with a guy named Adam (not his real name). We went for a walk along the beach for one of our dates. While we were walking, I commented, "I wonder where all the seagulls sleep at night?" Right away, Adam responded with, "They probably just sleep on the sand." I mentioned that a feral cat colony lived in the jetty that lined the sand and suggested that the cats may attack the seagulls if they were sleeping on the beach. Immediately, Adam responded, "Well then, they must sleep out on the ocean." I became overjoyed. I thought he was taking part in a verbal discourse like I was used to having with Carol, so I kept playing devil's advocate to each of the answers he came up with in hopes of keeping the game going. I likened it to a verbal volleyball game, and I wanted to see how many volleys in a row we could keep going before the ball hit the ground. I was thoroughly enjoying myself and utterly unaware that Adam was not having the same experience as I was.

At some point, I noticed Adam was starting to run out of answers when I disputed his. Adam had been such a good sport and had played along for much longer than I had expected. I wanted to wrap things up so Adam would not feel compelled to keep coming up with answers. Back then, Google and Siri were futuristic concepts that were not available to us yet. So, I referred to the next best thing. We had a mutual friend, Bodhi (not his real name), the brightest person I knew. He was like a walking encyclopedia (or Wikipedia for you younger ladies). I could go to Bodhi to ask him anything because he always had an answer. I was sure that one or more of the answers that Adam had already come up with were probably correct. However, since I had no factual knowledge about the sleeping habits of seagulls, I said, "I'll call Bodhi tomorrow and find out where the seagulls usually sleep." I thought Adam would be just as excited as I was to find out the answer. Adam got quiet after that, but I just figured he was tired from all the verbal volleyball we had just played. I sincerely did not realize I had offended him until the next time we went on a walk.

On our next walk, I was excited for another game of verbal volleyball. I quickly tossed out a question and was immediately slammed down by Adam's response: "I don't know. Why don't you call Bodhi." The tone of his voice shifted, and it was clear he was not happy with me. I genuinely had no idea why he was so upset. I was only sure that there would be no more verbal volleyball games with Adam.

I thought Adam and I were having a great time communicating. I did not understand that when I made the statement, "I wonder where all the seagulls sleep at night?" Adam had interpreted this statement as a problem he could solve for me. Each answer Adam contributed was his effort to provide me with a solution to my problem. Each time I countered one of his "solutions," he interpreted it as me shooting down his competency to solve my problem. I honestly thought we had experienced the same enjoyable verbal exchange. However, without even knowing it, I was wounding him with my words. When I dismissed his solutions, he felt rejected by me. I would never have intentionally said something to hurt Adam, yet I was ignorantly saying things that made Adam feel criticized and incompetent. My ultimate ignorance was apparent when I ended the conversation by saying that I would call Bodhi to obtain the answer to where the seagulls slept. I had no idea what a low blow I had hurled with this comment. I thought I was seeking a resolution to the game to vindicate Adam for all the good answers he introduced. Instead, Adam experienced my statement as the final insult to his competency by deeming Bodhi the utmost authority. I blatantly disrespected Adam, unknowingly.

It is essential to point out that it did not matter that I delivered my words with good intentions. Unfortunately, despite my best intentions, I still caused Adam pain due to my ignorance of the concepts shared in this chapter.

A Hidden Vulnerability

I had no idea why Adam's mood turned a bit icy on our second walk. Maybe you have no clue why you're getting the same reaction from your guy when you ask certain questions. I want to unravel this mystery for you so you don't unintentionally cause your guy harm, as I did to Adam.

Adam came across as very confident and strong. He was educated, hard-working, and had started his own business when he was in his twenties. Due to his success and self-confidence, I had no idea what was hidden beneath the surface.

> "A man's deepest fear is that he is not good enough or that he is incompetent."[1(p56)]

In a national survey of 400 men, three-fourths admitted that they are not always as confident as they look.[9] Regardless of how successful they were, they could appear very confident on the outside and still feel insecure just under the surface. For example, where a woman may ask the question, "Am I loveable?" a man will secretly ask, "Am I good enough?"

Men Question Their Competency

Many women are attracted to a man's strength and self-confidence with no awareness of his ongoing self-doubt and insecurity beneath the surface. Unfortunately, the magnitude of that self-doubt is greater than most women realize.[10]

The hidden vulnerability that rocks him to his core is the self-doubt that continually questions whether he is good enough. Anything that challenges whether he measures up as a boyfriend, husband, father, provider, etc., will be a tender spot for him. You will know when you have touched that raw nerve because you will either feel the chill when he turns icy or the heat when he turns angry. It is at this point in a conversation when conflict is most likely to erupt. He reacts to being deeply hurt. You become reactive because his response doesn't feel justified since you were not (knowingly) trying to hurt him. Without understanding the dynamic taking place beneath the surface, you will continue to engage in fights without ever comprehending what set them into motion.

How You See Him Matters a Lot

You may be unaware of how much he yearns for you to view him as competent at what he does – as a boyfriend, husband, father, provider, etc. Consequently, he is looking to you regularly for the answer to "Am I good enough?" So when he feels admired or appreciated by you, it breathes new life into his soul. Likewise, when he detects your lack of approval or unhappiness with him, it chips away at his very core.

Here is an example from my private practice that illustrates this point:

A client went out with her friends for a few hours while her husband watched their seven-month-old son. Upon arriving home, she found her husband and son sitting on the couch watching the baseball game. She made a sarcastic remark about how much her son must be enjoying the game.

That evening, she saw her husband watching the news in the living room. She took that opportunity to ask if their son could join him while she got some laundry done before bath time. She detected some frostiness in his tone when he replied, "No, I don't think he'll enjoy the news."

The wife was upset when she first arrived home because her expectation was that she would find her husband actively playing with their son. But her comment did nothing to increase her husband's desire for quality time spent with his son. The husband admitted during the session that he felt she was criticizing his competency as a dad. He wholeheartedly wants to be a good father, but he struggles with never-ending doubt that he'll be good enough as a first-time dad. When his wife made that sarcastic remark, he took her words as confirmation of his incompetence as a father. Just think how different things would have played out if the wife had been aware of his hidden self-doubt.

In contrast, consider how he would have felt about himself as a dad if she had walked through the door and exclaimed, "Looks like our son may grow up to share your love of baseball, or he just loves spending time with his dad!"

Your guy is human, and he wants to feel appreciated just like you do. But in a much deeper way, he *needs* to feel you see him as worthy and competent.[11] Unfortunately, he will probably be the last one to admit that. It may be too vulnerable for him to acknowledge and talk about it openly. Few things can crush his self-confidence faster or more severely than when he senses you lack trust in his abilities.

He Takes Your Unhappiness Personally

The sense of inadequacy that makes many men feel vulnerable may explain why he has difficulty listening to you when talking about your problems. He wants to make you happy, and when you express dissatisfaction or discontent over something, he feels like a failure. He incorrectly assumes that your mood is based solely on his behavior. He is quick to take credit when you are happy, but he equally takes responsibility when you are unhappy. He personalizes your unhappiness and then concludes that his deepest fear is valid: he really is not good enough.[1] His inability to make you happy leads him to feel incompetent.

For example, say you both had to work remotely from home during the COVID-19 pandemic and trying to set up two home offices in limited space was not ideal. On one particularly frustrating day, you vent about how much nicer it would be to have your own dedicated home office. What he hears is, "If you were a better provider, I wouldn't be stuck in this home that is making me miserable. You have failed me."

That's why it's so crucial to grasp how he internalizes your unhappiness. As women, we vent whenever we need to relieve stress and let go of things on our minds. Without being aware, you could be sending messages to him during your venting sessions that deeply hurt him. On the other hand, when you have this awareness, you can be a little more sensitive. Here are two alternative approaches that would not leave him feeling inadequate:

- You have worked so hard to provide us with this home and I still love it. Some days it's just so hard to carry on a Zoom meeting with all the noise in the background. I am longing to return to the office.

- I am so frustrated with working at home, and I just need to vent about how infuriating it is at times. I love you and I am not blaming you for anything that is about to come out of my mouth. Just let me vent and I'll feel better soon.

Unsolicited Advice Is Not Helpful and Can Be Hurtful

You pass out unsolicited advice every time you give a suggestion or helpful tip that he did not request. I trust that you are just trying to be helpful when you offer advice. Unfortunately, many men may perceive this differently, and your words can hurt them. If he has asked you for your advice, then it is perfectly acceptable to offer it. It is only a mistake when you offer *unsolicited* advice.

If you find your guy shutting down when you have tried to help, offer advice, or improve him, there is a high likelihood that he interprets this as offensive. It is similar to how you feel when you are sharing and are just looking for a listening ear and some support, and he tries to "fix" you or provide a solution to your problem. He feels just as offended when you try to "help" or "improve" him by offering unsolicited advice. His interpretation of your unsolicited advice is that you do not trust him anymore, which causes him to feel unloved.[1]

Caring Versus Trusting

Women are typically the nurturing ones in the relationship. Our intuition enhances our nurturing ability because it allows us to sense when someone is hurting and needs support. Therefore, offering help or assistance to a close girlfriend is welcomed as a loving gesture. It is not offensive, and there is no requirement to ask for permission first. Likewise, close female friends freely impart advice and offer suggestions to one another because these are signs of caring.

Since you are accustomed to this female culture, it may be hard to conceive that your guy may be reactive to you offering advice. While you may feel loved and valued when someone offers to help you, the same act can leave him feeling weak, incompetent, and even unvalued.[1] You may only want the best for him and share something hoping that it will help him grow. Instead, it may deprive him of his dignity because he believes you are telling him he is defective.

Most women value acts that communicate caring. We typically express acts of caring in a manner similar to how we appreciate receiving them from others. Unfortunately, the same action can convey something very different to a man. For example, say you are struggling to get a lid off of a jar. Then your guy asks, "Do you need help with that?" His comment would feel caring. You would appreciate his offer to assist you whether or not you needed his help.

On the other hand, say he has been wrestling with setting up the new artificial Christmas tree for a while. If you said to him, "Do you need help with that?" he may interpret your inquiry as you not trusting his ability to do it on his own. So instead of receiving your question as caring, he may actually be insulted by it. What feels like caring to him is when you trust him to take care of things independently and not offer assistance unless he asks for it. Of course, he may eventually request your help, but not until he has done everything he can on his own.

How He May Perceive You When You Offer Unsolicited Advice

Understanding his disdain for unrequested advice is vital for you to grasp because you can continue to unintentionally offend and cause harm while genuinely just trying to love and care for him. When you provide unsolicited comments or suggestions that you feel are helpful, here are various ways he may perceive you[12]:

- Unsupportive
- Unempathetic
- Distrusting
- Domineering
- Misunderstanding
- Assuming
- Questioning
- Arrogant
- Judgmental
- Condescending

Without understanding how he internalizes it, you may continue to offer unsolicited advice based solely on your intentions. It will not matter what your intent was when the result is him shutting down or becoming angry. The outcome will be disconnection, which is the direct opposite of the closer connection that you desire. Regardless of how good your advice is, it will be an obstacle to meaningful communication in your relationship if it is unwelcomed.

Unsolicited Advice From a Man's Perspective

One blogger shared what he hears when someone offers unsolicited advice. It might be eye-opening to hear this from a man's perspective:

I think you're inadequate and incompetent, and you require my superior knowledge and wisdom to make progress here. Without my help and intervention, you are a helpless victim incapable of dealing with your own problems. You should feel lucky that I'm even putting in my precious time and effort to give you some assistance. Furthermore, I don't accept you the way you are. I'm making it my mission to change you so that you fit into my idea of who I think you should be instead of accepting you as you are.[13]

If your guy feels anything remotely like this, it will have an adverse impact on your communication. It could also be contributing to why he has stopped listening and you no longer feel heard.

What Is the Outcome of All Your Invaluable Unsolicited Advice?

Advice can be beneficial when he asks for it. When it is not welcomed, the undesired effect may:

- Shut down conversation
- Create distance between the two of you
- Chip away at his self-confidence
- Stop him from trusting you
- Undermine his ability to make good decisions
- Ultimately leave you feeling lonely and unheard

Unsolicited Advice – Criticism in Disguise?

When you offer unsolicited advice that pertains to him or his behavior, it may feel like criticism in disguise. It morphs into criticism when the advice becomes frequent minor corrections. If you are saying any of the things below, you may not be aware that these fall into the category of unsolicited advice and may feel like criticism to him. They may seem harmless to you, but they could be annoying to him. If he is experiencing comments like these as criticism, then resentment will start to accumulate. Over time, he will begin to check out and be less inclined to hear you.

- Did they say our table won't be ready for 30 minutes? I thought you made a reservation.
- How long ago since your last haircut?
- I don't know how you can think in here. This place is a mess.
- I'll just call a handyman. He will know how to fix it.
- Don't order the fries. All that grease is bad for your heart.
- Those shoes should go in the next Goodwill bag.
- You're going to be late because you didn't leave enough time again.
- Why are you buying that? Don't you have one or two of those already?

- Your mom called again. When are you going to call her back?
- You just missed that parking spot. Maybe you can turn around and still get it.
- Where's the shirt I bought you that matches those pants better?
- When are you going to start going back to the gym?
- Why haven't you earned a raise lately?

Ask Permission First

A straightforward way to get around giving unsolicited advice is to ask permission first. He may still not be thrilled to hear your feedback, but you will have a better chance of being heard if he willingly agrees to listen to you. So, the next time you get that intuitive nudge and want to share your thoughts, ask permission before you reveal them. Here are some options of how to do so[14]:

- I have some thoughts about what might be beneficial. Are you interested in hearing them?
- Will you allow me to share some practical suggestions?
- I have experienced something similar. Let me know if you would find it helpful for me to share what worked for me.
- Are you open to feedback?

Practice Not Offering Unsolicited Advice

Even if you can see he's headed down a difficult road and your input could save him misery, let him work through his own problems and issues. Resist the urge to offer unrequested guidance. Unless he asks for your help, support him by keeping your thoughts to yourself as he figures it out on his own.

You have a choice. Would you rather:

1. Have a deep connection with him, or . . .
2. Have the awareness that he is harboring feelings of resentment toward you for your continual unwanted advice

See him as the expert of his own life. When you express confidence in him, it will be music to his ears. Not only will he appreciate you for that, but it will also cause his self-confidence to increase. Your belief in him is vital to his sense of competency. He will feel respected and supported when you can trust that the answers lie within him. Each time you believe he is capable of accomplishing things on his own without your input, he will feel your love deeply because he will know that you accept him for who he is and how he differs from you.

The goal is not for you to shut up and never offer any advice ever again. The goal is to regain his trust so that he welcomes your input. By you ceasing to dispense unwelcomed advice, your restraint will communicate respect. To feel your respect, he must believe that you trust him to make good decisions on his own. It may be necessary for you to let go of some control by being okay with letting him do things his own way. You'll have to accept that there is not only one way to do things right and stay calm when he doesn't do them in line with your schedule.

You will not lose yourself or your power when you stop freely dispensing insight into his life that he doesn't want or need. It may seem contrary, but as you restrain from readily sharing advice that he doesn't ask for, he will be inclined to value your opinion and insights even more. It will increase his trust in you, which will lead to a deeper attraction and connection. By choosing to share respectfully when asked, he will place you in a position of influence in his life. Ultimately, he will seek out your thoughts because he will want to hear what you have to say.

How Appreciation Combats Self-doubt

We've explored how a man routinely questions whether he is good enough. That self-doubt creates a deep need to be noticed and appreciated for what he does. Even if he never admits to it, when you acknowledge something your guy has done and genuinely thank him for it, that's when he feels especially cared for. For example, "Thank you for sitting through dinner quietly even though I know my mother drives you crazy."

How long you've been together doesn't matter. His desire to be appreciated and hear a simple "thank you" remains constant.

Do you think highly of your guy and have the utmost appreciation for the things he does for you, but rarely verbalize it? It is not good enough to assume he knows you appreciate him. It has no meaning unless he hears it from you. Unfortunately, it's common to take the person that means the most to you for granted from time to time. Be that as it may, once this occurs regularly, it can lead to resentment and diminish his motivation to carry out those generous deeds that further the relationship. It is vital to his well-being and your relationship as a whole for him to feel you notice his efforts.

Being Appreciated Is More Meaningful to Him Than You May Realize

Without understanding just how important it is to a man to feel appreciated, you may become frustrated at having to thank him for things you think he should just be doing. After all, you probably don't expect a thank you each time you do your routine tasks.

To gain perspective, think about how important it is for you to hear him say, "I love you." Would you be okay if he believed he shouldn't have to keep telling you because you ought to *know* he loves you? I doubt it. Even if you know he loves you, it does your heart good to hear him willingly verbalize it. That's equivalent to what your guy feels when you say "thank you."[40]

When you say "thank you," it communicates many things to him:

- Well done
- You take care of me
- You are important to me
- I value you
- I notice you
- I appreciate you

Instead of seeing his need to be thanked as petty, see it as a way to communicate love to him. When you screw up, you still want to know that he loves you. Likewise, when he is unable to meet your expectations, he still needs to know that you appreciate him.

For example, say you ask him to fix the vacuum cleaner and he is unable to. He will undoubtedly feel bad because he was unsuccessful. Consider how meaningful these words would be to him during a time he is experiencing failure: "Thank you for trying to fix the vacuum cleaner. I appreciate that even when you determined it was dead beyond repair, you spent extra time trying to breathe new life into it."

Coming from a sincere place, look for opportunities to appreciate him for the big things he does, the small things, and especially the imperfect things. Saying "thank you" isn't about whether he achieved the desired outcome. It's about acknowledging his willingness and effort instead of failures. He will feel encouraged when you recognize his worth in spite of imperfection.

Think about which scenario touches your heart more:

> You are dressed impeccably for a fund-raiser and have had your hair and make-up done professionally – he says, "I love you."

> You have been up all night with the baby teething, have throw-up on your shirt, and can't remember when you last showered – he says, "I love you."

Clearly, in the second scenario, you are not feeling as lovely as in the first, so his words have a more significant impact. Keep that in mind when your guy fails to meet one of your expectations. Instead of being quick to point out what wasn't accomplished (which I assure you he is fully aware of), take a minute to appreciate him regardless of the end result. He will be much more eager to take on the next task when he knows you will value his effort without criticism, even when he falls short.

Never bypass an opportunity to let him know you're proud of him

For some men, hearing "I am proud of you" can be more meaningful than hearing "I love you." You can simply say, "I am proud of you." However, I have provided additional options that shine a light on his hard work, talent, and character.

- I am so happy to be married to you – you're such a wonderful person
- I hope you know that I brag about you all the time when you're not around
- You repeatedly amaze me with your talent and accomplishments
- I respect you for doing the right thing because I know it wasn't easy
- You have earned every accomplishment you have achieved
- I never lacked confidence in your ability to accomplish this goal
- When you fix your attention to it, nothing stands in your way
- Our kids are fortunate to have you for a dad
- What an incredible accomplishment – you deserve a celebration
- I saw all the hard work you did, and it really paid off

- When I witness how you inspire others, I feel proud to be your wife
- You outdid yourself this time – what new strategy did you implement?
- You never cease to impress me with all that you can do

Mistake #2 – Top Takeaway Tips

♥ Carefully chosen words can curtail the casualty of him feeling incompetent

♥ Resist the urge to give unsolicited advice

♥ Take time to show ample appreciation

Mistake #3

A Mistake That Leads to False Assumptions

It is a mistake to assume you know what he meant when he said or did something that hurt your feelings. It is also a mistake to presume you know his intent.

Clueless Versus Malicious

Be assured that most men do not wake up plotting how they will make you miserable that day. More often than not, he is clueless, not malicious.

By clueless, I do not mean stupid. I have seen brilliant men make thoughtless remarks that upset their wives and girlfriends without realizing the impact of their words. Since he does not think like a woman, he has no idea how his words affect you. In his mind, if someone said the same thing to him, he would not be bothered by it, so he cannot understand why you are so disturbed. That is why it is imperative to let him know.

If he says something that hurts your feelings, tell him directly instead of just registering the hurt on your face and staying silent, hoping that he will get the message and acknowledge your feelings. You could say, "Ouch, that remark hurt. I interpreted it to mean (explain what your interpretation is). Is that what you meant?" Stay open to hear what he was trying to communicate instead of holding on to your conclusion. There is an enormous possibility that you will discover your interpretation of what he meant and how he meant it is genuinely different. He will often be caught entirely off guard when he realizes he hurt you. Then you have an opportunity to see that he was not being malicious and ignoring your feelings; he was simply unaware of them (clueless).

Cannonball Versus Belly Flop

One of my favorite past times is spending time in the sun reading a good book. I prefer to sunbathe at the beach because I love being cooled off by an ocean breeze while baking in the sun. However, there was a period of time that I lived in a condo complex that had two resort-style swimming pools, and it did not make sense to drive down to the beach when I was within walking distance from two amazing pools. You might be thinking, "That's nice, but what does this have to do with anything?" Hang in there. I will make a point that is relevant to the content of this chapter.

The drawback to laying out by the pool was when someone splashed water on my book (this occurred years before I had my waterproof Kindle). I enjoy taking good care of my books, so it would disturb me when they got wet. There were usually two scenarios that led to unwelcomed water coming my way. The first was a guy doing a cannonball. In my mind, the only purpose in doing a cannonball is to see how big of a splash you can make. Therefore, I became irritated quickly when a cannonball was done right by the edge of the pool I was lying near because there was always plenty of pool area nowhere near me. The second scenario involved someone diving into the pool, and due to not being angled enough as they entered the water, they ended up doing a belly flop, which created quite a splash. In the second scenario, I inevitably felt sorry for the person, not anger or irritation, because I realized it was not intentional. Unfortunately, the outcome was the same in both situations - my book ended up wet. However, the belly flop did not upset me because I deemed it unintentional.

I shared this story with you to give you a word picture of the clueless versus malicious concept. When your guy says something that hurts you, how often do you perceive his intent as a cannonball instead of a belly flop?

The result of you feeling hurt is the same, but your anger and frustration will be considerably less if you see it as a belly flop – him trying to do the best he can and unintentionally messing up.

The next time he says something that upsets you, try to picture him doing a belly flop. Most likely, that will give you enough time to hit the pause on the "quick to react" button. Then, from that place of giving him the benefit of the doubt that he did not intentionally try to upset you, you can decide if it is something you can voluntarily let go of. If not, you will be in a much better place to seek to understand what he meant. Since you did not overreact, you can ask him with a sincere sense of curiosity rather than go at him with an accusation – "What were you thinking when you said . . . ?" versus "What were you thinking!"

Word Pictures

Did having the word picture of a belly flop help illustrate the concept of him being clueless versus malicious? If it furthered your ability to retain that concept, you might consider using word pictures as another way to be heard.

In their book, *The Language of Love*, Dr. Gary Smally and Dr. John Trent explain how powerful word pictures are and teach you how to craft your own word pictures.

Trent defines what a word picture is:

An emotional word picture is a communication tool that uses a story or object to simultaneously activate the emotions and intellect of the listener. In so doing, the listener experiences your words, not just hears them. In short, when you use a word picture to communicate what you're trying to convey, it can go right through your spouse's defenses and straight into his (or her) heart.[15]

Word pictures are a language that men can understand. Often one word picture can penetrate barriers, whereas a wordy conversation may essentially fortify his barricades. If you have tried communicating countless times about something important to you and still do not feel heard, stop with all the words and try a "picture" to see if that will have a more significant impact. Trent has graciously offered a free PDF, "101 Life-Tested Word Pictures,"[16] on his website.

Personalize the Message

Another way you can enhance your communication style so he can hear you is to personalize it specifically for your guy. For example, instead of stating, "You hurt my feelings," you could say, "Remember how you felt when your dad told you (insert something that had an emotional impact on him)?" Give him a few seconds to connect with those feelings and then say, "That's how I felt after you told me (tie it back to what he said that hurt your feelings)." Sharing in this manner has a more significant impact on him. By relating your pain to a hurt he has personally experienced, you have created a bridge that allows him to connect with how you are feeling.

One of my clients shared how frustrated she was with her husband always making major decisions in the relationship and not allowing her to have any input. I knew that the couple had a daughter together and that the daughter was the apple of her daddy's eye. With that in mind, I suggested that the next time this situation occurred, to calmly say to her husband, "Honey, do you want our daughter to marry a man who completely dominates her and doesn't allow her to participate in the relationship? What if we begin to model the kind of relationship we want her to have so she will be more equipped to choose a man that respects her as a person and allows her to have a voice?" Enough said. He may not change at that moment, but I do not doubt that he heard her comment and that it'll get him thinking about it later, unlike the many yelling fights tried in the past.

Another client had been trying to get her husband to go to individual counseling for years to deal with past hurt he had bottled up inside, preventing him from connecting with her. No matter how hard she pushed him to do it, he would not budge. Then one day, my client said to her husband, "When our daughter gets to the age where she wants to have a heart-to-heart talk with her dad, are you going to be able to open up with her?" She said nothing more, and the next day, he never mentioned their conversation, but she saw him sitting at the computer and searching for therapists in the area. By forming the question in that manner, she personalized the situation enabling him to see himself as a good father seeking therapy to enhance his relationship with his daughter, rather than a lousy partner who needed help. She never called him a bad husband, but it is possible that every time she brought up him going to therapy, his perception was that she believed he was a failure as a husband.

Making Assumptions Is Harmful to Your Relationship

Assumptions are destructive and can severely damage your relationship. An assumption is something that is conclusively believed as truth without any evidence. Assuming is the direct opposite of open communication. It is dangerous because you are making up your mind about him without his input. By not allowing him to share his side of the story, he will feel misjudged and disregarded.

Even though you care deeply about him and may know him better than anyone else, you still cannot decide what his intentions are. His intentions exist only in his heart and mind. They are hidden from you. You may be able to accurately state the facts of the situation, but you can't know his feelings and thoughts without him sharing them. If you assume you know his intentions, at best, you may be partially correct, and at worst, you may have it entirely wrong.

An integral part of resolving conflict involves understanding his intentions. However, a sizable amount of your arguments can be avoided by not incorrectly deciding you know his intentions before he can explain himself.

What do assumptions sound like?

- He works a lot, so it's obvious he doesn't consider me a priority.
- He didn't comment on my new haircut, so he must not like it.
- He hasn't said much today, so he must be upset with me.
- He keeps saying he forgot to do what I asked, but I think he's getting even with me.
- He's been really distracted for the past couple of days. Does he still love me?

If you make an assumption about him and do not take the time to clarify it, you are no longer in a relationship with him. Instead, you have moved into a relationship with that assumption.[17] When you bypass communication and become preoccupied with your assumptions, you will become lonesome because you have cut off a meaningful exchange with him, and your connection is severed. Conversely, your relationship will benefit significantly if you make the decision to assume nothing.

Mistaken Assumptions = Miscommunication

Mistaken assumptions might contribute to much of the miscommunication in your relationship.

Are these comments he has said to you?

- Stop telling me what I think.
- Stop putting words in my mouth.
- Stop assuming you know how I feel.

Are these the beginning of stories you tell yourself?

- I am certain he ...
- I have a feeling that he ...
- It's obvious that he ...
- I just know he ...

If so, you may want to acknowledge that making assumptions about him or his behavior could play a crucial role in the communication difficulties you two are experiencing. If you can identify any assumptions that you are currently holding onto that have been upsetting or disrespectful to him, start with an apology. Apologize to him for jumping to a conclusion without seeking his input. Then ask questions to understand and stay open to hearing something other than the conclusion you previously came to. If he sincerely hears your impartiality and vulnerability, it may open communication in a new way. However, if he sniffs out any judgment, the conversation will go nowhere.

Believing the Worst

Once you fall into the routine of making assumptions, it sparks the domino effect, and one assumption leads to another until you can no longer see the truth about your partner. The unfortunate reality is that once this happens, you will almost always believe the worst about him. The biggest reason this happens is that you conclude what his intentions are according to how his actions made you feel.[18] When you come to a conclusion based solely on your hurt feelings, you will inevitably assume the worse. Say he acted in a way that showed disregard for your emotions, and you conclude he doesn't care about your feelings. That verdict is established entirely on how you felt and left no consideration to what was going on with him.

Once you decide his intentions are bad, it is easy to leap to the conclusion that he is a bad person.[18] Now you are attacking his character, which will become the lens through which you judge all future behavior. If you presume he is an uncaring person, that judgment will affect your whole relationship. Instead of it being a conversation where you seek to understand his intention, this false assumption will sour the way you routinely interact with him.

Give him the benefit of the doubt – do not decide his intent until you seek to understand by asking questions. Initiate a discussion from a place of curiosity instead of judgment. Ask questions to figure out where he was coming from and be willing to hear that it may not be what you assumed. Please shift your perspective from "HOW COULD HE!" to "How could he?"

Past Pain Can Influence Your Reaction

It is necessary to point out that if you have unhealed pain from your past, it may influence how you react to hurtful things he says unintentionally. For example, did you have malicious people in your life who inflicted verbal assaults regularly? The people I am referring to are the ones who spew words peppered with poison with the intent to cause pain. It could have been a mom, dad, ex-husband, teacher, coach, etc.

When you have experienced that kind of cruelty, it can leave you feeling that any pain felt from someone else is intentional. If you have endured circumstances like that, I encourage you to acknowledge the hurt you have suffered and seek healing for the wounds inflicted in your past. Those are real wounds, and you would benefit from the attention of a professional who can come alongside you with care and compassion. I hope you are in a relationship with a decent man rather than an abusive one. If so, try to give him the benefit of the doubt when he rubs up against your past hurt. He probably is not doing it intentionally and has no idea how deep your pain truly is.

Please understand he is not responsible for the *depth* of your pain. That's because much of that pain is a response to your past. He is only accountable for the thoughtless statement he said that unintentionally triggered the past. It would be best not to deny the pain that surfaces because it is coming up to seek your attention and recovery. It has been lying in your past unattended to and uses these occasions to send you intense feelings to get your attention so you can realize that healing is necessary.

When you have an over-reaction to something he says or the reaction is way more intense than the actual situation called for, it is usually safe to say that a good portion of that reaction is a response to hurt from your past. When you understand this dynamic, you can take responsibility for it and respond more appropriately. He cannot make this better for you because he is not the author of this pain. You can help yourself and him by saying something like, "Ouch, when you said that, it triggered something deep from the past. In the future, it would help me if you would say it like this . . ." By shifting from a place of blaming him, to seeking his assistance instead, it opens the door for him to be better able to hear you and offer you his support.

3 Steps to Put an End to Making False Assumptions

The following steps will assist you in putting an end to making false assumptions:

1. **Take ownership.** You will continue to make assumptions, but you can start to recognize when it happens and take responsibility for it as soon as possible to avoid sitting in pain or inflicting harm.
2. **Open communication.** Start by asking yourself an important question: Without input, can I determine if this is 100% true? Undoubtedly, you will discover that it's impossible to know his intent without his feedback. Take time to have a conversation with him to understand what occurred from his point of view. Then, with affection and gentleness in your voice, ask questions to discover his motivations.
3. **Listen attentively without bias.** While listening to his comments on why he said or did what he did, stay open to hear his truth without running it through the filter of what you predetermined. Initially, you may want to reject what he says because it seems far removed from what you concluded. Instead, decide to receive his side of the story, even if it is hard to wrap your mind around. Try not to focus on being right. Preferably, use this time to gain a deeper understanding

of him. It won't take long before you discover that he seldom has an ulterior motive.

Why Can't He Just Speak My Language?

At this point, do you find yourself thinking: Why do I have to seek clarification for almost everything he says? Why can't he learn to speak my language?

As frustrating as it may get at times, the truth remains that you two are very different. You come from different backgrounds, you had different childhoods, your conversational styles are different, and the sheer fact that he is not a woman will impair your ability to understand his frame of reference. Thankfully, the time you invest in seeking clarification, rather than assuming, will provide you both with insight not previously known. Furthermore, that awareness will enhance your ability to develop effective communication where you both can be heard and understood.

Mistake #3 – Top Takeaway Tips

- ♥ Stay curious about his intent – seek to understand without assuming

- ♥ Consider whether he was clueless or malicious (bellyflop vs. cannonball)

- ♥ Try using word pictures to illustrate what you want to be understood

Mistake #4

A Mistake That Leads to Competitiveness

Many women make this mistake without even being aware they are creating distance from the man they love. You may think you are sharing comments to connect with him and have no idea that he is experiencing you as trying to compete with him. It happens a lot during dating and can be what causes a guy to lose interest early on. I also see this frequently occur with couples that have been together a long time.

Connecting Versus Competition

As women, we approach communication from a relational standpoint and engage with the purpose of connecting. For instance, when a girlfriend is sharing, and we can identify with it, we are quick to say "me too" and share a similar story as a way to mutually relate.

This is a customary way of communicating for most women because it feels good to establish a connection by finding a common link. As a result, it may be baffling to believe that this could be considered off-putting by a man.

In the male culture, they have grown up using communication to establish rank and negotiate their position of power.[19] Therefore, a man and a woman can be in the same conversation and come away with very unrelated interpretations of what took place due to their different reasons for engaging. For example, a man will evaluate a conversation by determining whether it left him in a one-up or one-down position from the other person. On the other hand, a woman will assess it by discerning whether it made her feel closer to or further from the other person.

How This Difference Plays Out

That is why when we meet a new guy, and he shares that he has recently been to ABC Snow Resort and we have been there too, we do not think twice before responding how much we love ABC Snow Resort and may even add how much we enjoyed eating at The High-End Restaurant in town. We might go on to inquire if he has been to XYZ Snow Resort because we love that one even better, and we want to see if he has ever been there. As we are talking, we feel excited because we believe that we have made a good connection over the love of skiing and traveling to the same places.

Unfortunately, we do not realize that he did not experience the conversation the same way. To him, it felt like we were competing with him by one-upping him. Men hate this. They deal with competition among their male friends and in the workplace. The last place they want to engage in competition is when they spend time with a woman they are interested in. What would have felt more engaging to him would have sounded something like, "Oh, I love ABC Snow Resort too. What's your favorite thing about skiing there?" Now he feels you are interested in what he's saying and knows you have been there too. He can continue sharing without being interrupted, and you have opened the opportunity for him to ask you questions about your shared interest.

By Understanding This Difference, You Can Find a Middle Ground

A client shared how she was discouraged with internet dating, and I discovered she had no idea she was stepping on landmines and blowing up conversations. She recounted a phone call she had with a guy. They were getting to know each other before the first date. It was going remarkably well because they had so much in common. The guy shared about a hiking trip he had recently been on. My client then shared about a hiking adventure she had done where two people almost died due to an avalanche while ascending to the summit. The guy stayed quiet while she shared all the shocking details. When she finished, he simply said, "Sounds like your hike was more dangerous than mine," and he hung up. She never heard from him again.

She had no idea what blew up the conversation. She chalked it up to, "he's just another jerk." Sadly, he may have been a really great guy, but she lost the opportunity to find out. After I explained to her what her comments felt like to him, she was able to see what transpired with new insight. She realized that he thought she was minimizing his experience because she brought up a grander story - one he could not compete with. She also grasped that by introducing her stories before she took the time to listen to him, she unintentionally gave the impression that she was more interested in herself than listening to him.

On her next date, she didn't shut down and refrain from sharing her stories. Instead, she remained mindful of avoiding these landmines by being present when the guy shared and not quickly launching into her stories. When she asked questions to learn more about him and his experiences, it conveyed that she cared about what he thought and him as a person. In turn, he was surprisingly eager to hear her stories too.

This Difference Can Show Up at Any Stage of the Relationship

This mistake also happens in long-term relationships. For example, say your husband expresses what a rough day he had at work and you immediately respond with, "My day was rotten too. Let me tell you what happened to me . . ." and you go on without even acknowledging his lousy day. I have watched many men get upset in my office when this happens because they feel their wife is minimizing their experience and not recognizing how hard they work. I know it is not your intent to one-up him, but your husband may not understand that you are just trying to connect. Instead, he may perceive you as posturing for dominance by describing how your day was worse.

You may have some meaningful things to share about your day, but if you enter that conversation as a piggyback to his, I guarantee there is little chance that he will hear them. Instead, let him finish sharing about his rough day. Start with acknowledging his feelings. Then, ask questions to gain understanding and show interest. Finally, only offer advice if he asks for it. Once his talking comes to an end, then you can share about your day. When he does not feel in competition with you, you are more likely to be heard.

It Is Also a Mistake to Compare Him to Other Men

You may not be aware of the effect you have on your guy when you compare him to another man. Also, you may not realize when you go on and on about another man being great at something that your guy hears, "Let me tell you what great looks like because you don't measure up." If you think that is petty on his part and he should get over it, consider it from another perspective. Say your guy starts to share about a friend of yours he saw at the last pool party. He comments on how amazing she looks in a bathing suit after having a baby. Even if you agree with his comment, it may ignite some of your own insecurities about your body image. All that to say, both of you have insecurities. If it feels respectful for him not to comment on other women's bodies, then kindly offer the same level of respect by not commenting on how good of a husband, boyfriend, dad, provider, etc. that other men are.

In this age of social media, drawing comparisons has taken on a life of its own. Too often, a woman will be sitting next to her guy, scrolling through social media, and making comments like:

- She gets flowers every Friday – her husband is amazing.

- Look at the jewelry he buys her – he really knows how to treat her like a woman.

- I can't believe they got into that restaurant – he only takes her to the most expensive places.

- Look at the color of the water in Belize. It's even nicer than when they were in Bali earlier this year. She's so lucky to be with a guy that loves to travel.

- Joe took the kids to the water park all day. Looks like they are having a blast. He's such a hands-on dad.

Men describe hearing their wives or girlfriends comparing them to other men as demoralizing.[20] Demoralizing is defined as causing someone to lose confidence or hope. For example, if your guy hears you making comments about how wonderful another man is, it could leave him disheartened and discouraged. That may lead to him pulling away or shutting down – both having the opposite effect on your desire to be heard.

You may unpremeditatedly comment aloud about another man, or you may make the comparison hoping to inspire your guy to improve his behavior or step up his game. Some men may rise to the challenge and start performing better to win your approval. Unfortunately, many will just become discouraged and stop trying. Please be mindful of how your guy responds and adjust your comments accordingly. I can tell you with certainty that you will have a better shot at motivating your guy by believing in him, respecting him, and having high expectations of him.

A Man's Competitive Nature Can Show Up in Many Aspects of His Life

I have shared instances of how the connection versus competition difference can impact your conversations. Although if a man observes interactions by who is one-up or one-down, it will show up in other aspects of his life. For example, driving is an area where some men's competitive nature may show up. I stumbled across this insight while I was driving with a friend. I was becoming a little uncomfortable because he was tailgating the car ahead of us. I asked him why he felt the need to be so close to that car's bumper. He said, "See that car out your side window? If I leave any room, he may try to get ahead of us and he'll take the lead." I laughed out loud because I thought he was kidding. Then I realized that he was dead serious. So, having some understanding of the competitive nature of men, I asked, "Do you imagine you are entering a contest every time you get behind the wheel?" "You bet," he replied. I found the whole concept fascinating because when I become aware of a driver needing to get over, I readily cooperate by giving them space. The thought that I would be "losing" that spot to another driver had never entered my mind. I had one final question, "Does it matter that the guy beside us doesn't know he is participating in this contest?" He quickly replied, "Trust me - he's in on it."

For the rest of the trip, I asked my friend to share out loud his driving strategy for the competition he was engaged in. It was intriguing to have a view into the male mind for a moment in time. Instead of simply driving across town, I felt like I was in an intense video game with live narration. I found it absolutely captivating. I would have been utterly unaware of everything going on in his head without his willingness to share his pursuit.

I share that story to illustrate how a man can be experiencing a situation from a competitive place while we are completely unaware. Understanding how differently some men observe an incident is key because it may lend some insight into why your guy reacts so strongly to something you had no idea could lead to conflict.

Mistake #4 – Top Takeaway Tips

- ♥ Understand that he may misinterpret your attempt to connect in conversation as you trying to one-up him

- ♥ Be mindful to not step on the landmines

- ♥ Avoid comparing him to other men

Mistake #5

A Mistake That Leads to Him Shutting Down

It is a mistake to talk to him like he is your girlfriend. It is tempting to chat with your guy like a girlfriend and expect him to listen as girlfriends do. You may consider him your best friend, but he is still not your girlfriend. The culture he grew up in did not utilize talking and sharing as an opportunity to nurture a relationship. Men are more likely to communicate when they want to share information or solve a problem.

Without understanding what makes him unique as a male, you may routinely interact with him like a girlfriend. In this chapter, I have summarized some of the ways women commonly talk. If you are sharing in this manner with your guy, it may be obstructing your ability to be heard.

Sue Shepard, MFT

The Devil Is in the Details

The idiom "the devil is the details" usually signifies that we should concentrate on the details and that even the most minor details matter. When talking to most men, using too many specifics is a mistake easily made. When women talk to other women, it is not uncommon to share every detail of a story because it builds intimacy. For that reason, it is understandable that you would do the same thing when talking to a man. It makes perfect sense that you feel that sharing the particulars will help him clearly understand what you are going through and draw you closer. Truthfully, most men would prefer that you get to the point.

Sharing the details of our lives or a problem we are experiencing is important to us as women. I am not trying to get you to change who you naturally are. I am just trying to propose a middle ground. The ideal midpoint is where you can continue to be who you are and talk in a fulfilling manner, but at the same time, do not give rise to him becoming frustrated and ultimately contribute to him no longer listening to you.

You can create this middle ground by letting him know at the beginning of the conversation what the final result will be and then go back and give the details. I love a story with a build-up because the tension adds to the overall enjoyment of the story. Unfortunately, many men do not enjoy the suspense because they have no idea where you are going in the conversation and can quickly become frustrated. You have a better chance of being heard if you avoid keeping him in suspense. Set your exchange up for success by letting him know the conclusion and then go back and give the details of how you ended up there.

Here are a couple of examples:

- I ended up deciding on *Tranquil Dawn* as the paint I will use in the family room. Let me tell you what I went through to get to that decision and all the headaches I encountered along the way.
- John and Mary had a healthy baby boy this morning. The outcome was good, but there were so many complications. Let me tell you what happened...

Be Careful to Not Talk for Too Long

More than a few women can get together and talk for hours, and it is effortless. On the other hand, most men consider communication as a means to an end and usually do not have the stamina for long, drawn-out conversations and will often just shut down. If you see him showing signs that he is getting bored or losing interest, it is time to wrap up the conversation. Your chances of being heard will improve if you approach the topic in a few short talks rather than a long discussion where he has already checked out. He will appreciate you keeping it brief, and if he wants to know more, he will ask.

Do you ever find yourself lengthening your conversation because you don't feel heard? Does your tone increase and your word count multiply? It is easy to fall into this pattern, but the result of you over-talking is him under-listening.[21] Talking when he has shut down guarantees that he will not hear any meaningful matter you are trying to convey. Since the goal is to feel heard, you will set yourself up for increased success by stating your point only once per conversation with the volume turned down. Give him time to take in the information and then revisit it at another time if it still needs to be addressed.

Talk About One Topic at a Time

If you start talking about one matter and it reminds you of something else, and you swiftly switch to a new issue and possibly to a third or fourth topic in the same discussion, your conversation has gone off on a tangent. I am highly skilled at tracking a tangential exchange like this because many people that come into therapy often talk in this fashion, especially in the beginning when they are nervous. Unfortunately, the average man does not have this skill. Men are usually more proficient at being single-focused. Your guy may not only get lost listening to this conversation, but it may also feel distressing and exhausting to him. Keeping in mind that it may take too much effort to follow your conversation, talk about one matter at a time if you want him to hear you.

Another reason he may get frustrated and stop listening to you when you cover multiple subject matters in one conversation is that his reference point may be one of logic and order. Therefore, he listens assuming the items you are sharing are delivered logically. Unfortunately for him, logic and order may not be your priorities while sharing your feelings. When you start changing from one topic to another or begin talking about one problem and then include several unrelated issues, he may become very exasperated. That is because he is logically trying to connect all the topics you have discussed. When he cannot understand how they all relate to one another, he may just stop listening.

Save Your Girl Talk for Your Girlfriends

Before you get angry at him for not listening, take a moment to check the topic of your conversation. It is an unacceptable expectation to count on him to be interested in everything you share with him. You would probably lose interest quickly if he went into minute detail about rebuilding his engine. If he started explaining each step he took to disconnect the external engine components, I suspect you would lose interest before he got to step three. Your lack of attention is directly related to the fact that the details of rebuilding an engine are not something you consider captivating. Not being interested in rebuilding an engine has no relevance to how much you love him or how interesting you find him.

Likewise, when you start talking about a subject typically reserved for your girlfriends, please do not get hurt when he starts to yawn without hiding it. Instead, when you see the yawn, be playful and crack a joke about his lack of enthusiasm in the subject and save the topic for one of your friends who will thoroughly enjoy hearing about it. There is nothing wrong with him or you if he is not entirely interested in every facet of your life. Embrace that you two are not the same person, and it is normal to have separate interests.

Stop, *Look*, and Listen

The excessive amount of time we spend looking at a screen has impacted our relationships. For example, every time I dine out, I am amazed at how many people are sitting across from one another and looking down at their phones instead of at each other. If you two have fallen into this trap, make a pact to keep phones face down on the table during meals or while trying to have a conversation. Agree to give each other your undivided attention. Sustaining eye contact with your partner creates closeness and connection during your exchange.

Decker teaches the difference between eye contact and eye communication. He states that eye contact is quick, often a mere glance for a split second.[22] On the other hand, eye communication maintains eye contact for at least 3-5 seconds. When your eyes look into his eyes and hold that gaze, true interconnectedness takes place.

Eye communication can be a splendid way to strengthen and deepen the bond between you two. When you each sustain eye contact with one another, your bodies release a small dose of Oxytocin.[23] Oxytocin, also known as the "love hormone," creates bonding and the feeling of being in love. For an investment of only 3-5 seconds, you are building trust and establishing emotional closeness.

The benefits of eye communication are[22]:

- Creates rapport between you two
- Increases your ability to influence and motivate him
- Strengthens his involvement as a listener
- Increases the likelihood of him remembering what you said[24]

The advantages listed above validate that you enhance your chances of being heard by practicing eye communication.

Multi-tasking and Communication Do Not Mix

Since multi-tasking comes easily to most women, we make the mistake of believing that all men can do the same. Some men do well at this, but many do not.

It is not atypical for a woman to be drafting an email she promised her boss while getting lunches made. At that same time, while ensuring the kids have everything they need to take to school, she can still add an item to the mental shopping list she has in her head. If this sounds like you, you will have a better chance of being heard if you stop your multi-tasking while talking to him and make sure you have his full attention too.

You may be busy in one room and yell something necessary to him in the other room. For example, say you asked him to pick up the dry cleaning on the way home. Do not be fooled by an "uh-huh" coming back from him because you could be setting the stage for a fight later when he arrives home without the dry cleaning.

The chances of him registering your words are severely compromised because there was no way to see if you had his full attention. Therefore, if you have something consequential to say or a request to make, avoid having the conversation when you are in a different room.

Walk into the room he is in and see what he is doing before you start talking. If he is reading the newspaper or looking at a screen (TV, computer, phone, etc.), the likelihood that he is taking in what you are saying is slim to none. Ask him to get rid of any distractions if you want to have a decent conversation. Once he puts down his phone or newspaper, closes the laptop, or mutes the TV, look him in the eye and keep steady eye contact to ensure you have his full attention.

Once you finally have his full attention, do not fall into the mistake of making multiple requests. Doing so will lessen the success of any of them getting done. Instead, only convey one topic or request at a time to maximize your chance of being heard.

A Trip to the Store

Another place you may encounter his single focus versus your ability to move from task to task is a trip to the store. For example, let's say you ask him to go with you to Home Depot because you want to replace the air filters in the house and you want his help picking out the correct filters. He readily agrees and is in a good mood until you place the filters in the cart and start heading to the garden department. You saw a sale sign when you walked in and decided to grab a couple of bags of plant food for your garden. On the way to the garden department, you see the light bulb aisle and make a sharp right to look for replacement bulbs for the guest bedroom lamp that went out last week. Of course, by now, he is no longer in a good mood and is huffing and puffing. You may even get mad at him at this point because you feel that he is acting like a child. Right here is where both of you have misinterpreted your differences, and judgment is rearing its ugly head.

There is no bad or wrong person in this scenario – only two different people. He is frustrated because you said you were going to Home Depot to get air filters. One goal. Therefore, when the air filters are in the cart, he deems the mission complete. However, when he sees you heading the shopping cart away from the check-out section, his sense of accomplishment evaporates quickly. His unhappiness is directly related to his difference from you. He prefers to pursue a specific outcome or a goal with a single focus. On the other hand, you are more comfortable switching between tasks and can handle more than one task simultaneously.

You two are different people who are not going to handle situations the same. The goal is not to make him like you or for you to become him. The goal is to be comfortable with him having an approach contrary to yours and making peace with his differences rather than judging him as wrong.

When you understand his difference, you can work with it better. For example, when you saw the sign for the plant food as you entered the store, that would have been a suitable time to say, "Oh look, they have plant food on sale, and I'm about to run out. Better stop at the garden shop on our way out." He still may not be happy that the plans have changed, but he will understand your logic for making that decision and hopefully have a little time to adjust from his single goal shifting to two.

Then when you remembered the burnt-out bulb that needed replacement, you could be playful and say something like:

> I just had a light bulb moment! The light in the guest bedroom died last week, and I don't have any spare bulbs for that lamp. I appreciate your flexibility and willingness to stop at the garden shop on the way out. I don't mean to take advantage of your kindness, so I'll be quick as I grab a pack of replacement bulbs.

He will probably make some grumbling noises. Just kiss him on the cheek and say, "You're the best!" The key is not to take his grumble personally or decide he's flawed because he is not delighted about the detour. When you encounter these situations that highlight your differences, try to observe them as unique traits rather than points of contention.

Forgetfulness Might Indicate That He Does Not Actually Hear the Information

Are you in the habit of giving your guy multiple tasks to do and find yourself often irritated because they aren't getting done? It is possible that when you are expressing several things you want him to take care of, he only hears the first or last item on the list. Everything else does not even register in his brain. If the following conversation is familiar to you, then this dynamic is probably occurring in your relationship:

> You: Why haven't you done this yet?
>
> Him: You never asked me to do that.

It can feel like he is selectively listening or completely tuning you out. However, it could also result from his brain not recording the entire list of your requests. If you have an ongoing problem with him forgetting to do things you ask him to do, start with just asking for one thing at a time and see if that helps. If not, maybe you can present the problem to him by saying, "Would you work with me to find a better way for me to communicate requests to you so they will be easier to remember?" Now the two of you can join forces to help identify a solution.

Some options you may toss around are:

- Email – if he is always on email and used to getting requests at work via email, he may also elect to have you send emails. He may have a flagging system that he already uses to highlight important emails and mark them with priority.

- Text – many of my clients elect to send and receive tasks and To-do's via text and usually want minimal words, preferable in bullet form. If there are too many words, you risk that he might not read the full text and increases the likelihood that you may only get a portion of what you wanted.

- Written note – he may prefer the old-fashioned written note. If you chose this method, be sure you both agree on a spot where all messages will be left so the paper can be easily seen, not overlooked, and other items will not keep it from being visible.

- Whiteboard – some clients utilize a whiteboard as a message center instead of a written note that can get lost. He can always take a picture of the message on the whiteboard, so he has it on his phone. For example, a couple was going through a remodel, which caused enormous stress in their relationship. She was the more detailed-oriented person who never let a task go unfinished or missed a deadline. But so many of the decisions required her husband's expertise and needed him to speak with the general contractor, Joe. So, she devised a whiteboard and only put items on it that required his immediate attention. For example, "Electrical problem. Call Joe tomorrow." "Decision needed on door sizes. Call Joe before Monday." Her husband committed to checking the board before leaving the house every day and when he got home each night. Instead of contacting him throughout the day, she only reached out if a problem arose after he left for the office and needed a response before he got home. It relieved an enormous amount of her stress and her husband no longer felt continually interrupted at work during the day.

- App – if he is technically savvy, he may prefer to use an app. Many of my clients have used "Remember the Milk," available for IOS and Android. It is an excellent To-Do App for busy people. They have a free version that is especially useful and a paid version with all the bells and whistles. You can add tasks on the free version using Alexa, Google Assistant, and Siri, and the paid version integrates with the Apple watch. Many wives have expressed that they like adding items to his to-do list because the app will take over reminding him via text or email.

Mistake #5 – Top Takeaway Tips

♥ Avoid keeping him in suspense → start with the conclusion

♥ Multi-tasking + Communication = Miscommunication

♥ Save your girl talk for your girlfriends

Mistake #6

A Mistake That Leads to Unsuccessful Conversations

It is a mistake to just launch into a conversation with a man without setting the stage for success.

You may not even be aware that this is a mistake because most women can easily switch into talk mode when a friend needs to talk. For example, you may have had a girlfriend that you could call at 2:00 AM to lament over a recent break-up. It may have woken her up, but she could start to empathize with you within five seconds. But if you tried to wake up your guy at 2:00 AM to talk about something important, it could feel like a jolt to his system. He would probably feel somewhat disoriented and possibly even mad.

The thing is, even if it's not 2:00 AM, it sometimes feels like a jolt to his system when you want to talk about something important, and he is not prepared. Being able to speak to another woman at a moment's notice is probably something you are used to. For that reason, it would be easy to assume your guy should be able to do the same. But, even though this may come naturally to many women, just as many men cannot do this effortlessly, and expecting them to do so, is a mistake.

Timing is Everything

Many women make the mistake of trying to have a meaningful conversation with their guy during the first few minutes he walks through the door or calling him right when he gets off work. Numerous men have sat in my office and said they need at least 20 to 30 minutes from when they walk through the door to switch out of work mode and transition into home mode.

Needing transition time is not just necessary for men. Most of my working clients (male and female) express their need for time to decompress before engaging in a serious conversation. If you are attempting to communicate something important to him during this time frame, there is a high likelihood you will not feel heard, and if you are, only a portion of what you said will get through.

The need for time and the amount of time needed will differ for each man. So ask your guy if he is someone that would benefit from having time to transition from work. Then find out how much time he needs so you can be supportive. Sometimes his need and your needs will conflict. For example, maybe he needs 30 minutes to unwind after work, but you need his help to watch the kids if you're trying to get dinner on the table. Instead of getting into an argument over whose needs are more significant, present it as a problem and solicit his help in finding a solution. For example, try saying something like this:

> I want to respect your need for 30 minutes to unwind after arriving each evening, but if we're going to eat by 6:00, I need your help watching the kids. Will you please work with me to find a solution that meets both of our needs?

With this approach, both of your needs have equal priority. Together, you two can reach an agreement that allows each of you to respect one another rather than it becoming a fight where someone ends up feeling their wants were devalued or discounted.

IT Guy Shares a Helpful Analogy

During a couple's session where the husband was complaining about his wife bombarding him with a series of topics the minute he walked through the door, he shared what it was like for him:

> My wife rapid fires topics at me as I walk through the door. First, she'll tell me something that happened with the kids, then about a large purchase we need to decide on, then ask when is a good day to get together with friends. I realize her questions are necessary to discuss, but I can't take in and process a response to any of them. In my IT job, I take in an enormous amount of data daily. To take in more data, I first have to offload some of that input before taking in what my wife tells me. I liken it to a full flash drive. In order to be able to put more data on the flash drive, I have to delete or transfer data to free up space. I need 30 minutes when I first arrive home to sort through the daily data and determine what I can let go of so I have room for more data from my wife. I think my wife gets frustrated when she gives me some time and sees me watching TV or tinkering in the garage. She may feel that I am choosing to do those things rather than talk to her, but she doesn't realize that I am offloading the excess data from my day as I do those mindless tasks.

This explanation made perfect sense to his wife, and she started giving him the first 30 minutes to himself when he arrived home. She admitted that sometimes it was tough not to interrupt him as he enjoyed himself in front of the TV when she had pressing things to discuss. Instead, she reminded herself that he processed his day differently and she chose to hold back. When she interrupted him, she could see he was never fully listening. By waiting, she finally felt heard.

Working From Home

It is essential to acknowledge that more and more people have begun to work from home. Working remotely blurs the lines even more because there is no longer the commute from the office and walking through the door. Instead, he may simply walk out of the other room or close his laptop in the same room. As a result, establishing a time frame acceptable to both of you for the transition from work to home is needed more than ever. As you will see in the following case, it is also essential to set clear boundaries for the workday.

I had a session with a couple still adapting to working at home due to the COVID-19 lock-down. The husband is a teacher who had to transition from the classroom to teaching remotely via Zoom, which also involved developing an appropriate curriculum for remote instruction. Of course, another part of his day involved grading homework and communicating with students and their parents. He explained that he goes into the zone while working in his home office and does not want to be interrupted until he emerges. The wife is a fashion designer and has a more flexible schedule. Part of her creative process is taking breaks throughout the day and in between projects. During her idle time, she often tries to engage her husband, and what began as minor frustrations ultimately erupted into a huge fight which landed them in my office. She did not understand his need to remain single-focused and stay in the zone. Therefore, she felt she was being helpful by introducing a little fun into his day and encouraging work-life balance by trying to coax him out of the office to have lunch with her.

The husband described how in all the years he had taught on campus, his routine was to arrive early before the students came to prepare for the day's instruction because once class started, he wanted to fully engage with the students. The time allotted for lunch primarily consisted of getting work done at his desk or talking to a colleague about work while maybe nibbling on something not too distractive. He said that he could not remember a time he left the classroom to go somewhere and just eat and that this was true for most of his colleagues on campus. That is why he became so frustrated when his wife kept trying to get him to join her in the kitchen for lunch. In addition, he had become very resentful of all her interruptions throughout the day.

He understood that taking breaks helped his wife be more creative, but the gaps were counterproductive for him because they took him out of his "zone" and interrupted his flow of thinking. He thoroughly explained what it was like for him to refocus once he lost his train of thought, and she finally understood that what she meant with only good intentions was surpriseingly disturbing to him. He apologized for blowing up, and she was able to commit to not interrupting him during his workday unless there was an emergency.

It is critical to point out that when the wife was stubbornly holding on to her position of being right because she was only trying to help him, she was unable to see that her actions were affecting him adversely regardless of her intentions. She did not believe he had a reason to be upset, so she would not listen to him (until they came into my office).

With that in mind, please take a moment the next time he gets very upset about something you feel is unwarranted. Before you pass judgment or polarize your point of view, genuinely try to grasp why he is so upset. It will not mean that you intentionally did anything wrong, but like the couple above, most miscommunication that results in conflict rarely results from something done deliberately. This book's predominant theme is that most miscommunication is due to a lack of understanding of each other's differences, so always err on the side of seeking to understand where he is coming from. Hopefully, he will begin to do the same.

Begin with the End in Mind

It will benefit both of you if you let him know what you would like from him before you even begin to talk. Foremost, the expectation will not be for him to "know" what you want and end up penalized for failing miserably. Furthermore, you have a considerably better chance of feeling heard and getting what you want when you start in this manner.

Here are some options of what you may ask for:

- Just to vent
- Need a solution
- Need a hug
- Want to brainstorm the situation and come up with my own solution
- Want his feedback
- Do not want his feedback

Say you want to brainstorm, but you want to come up with your own solution. Here is one example of what you could say:

> I've narrowed it down to three options I am considering. I would like to talk through those with you, but I do not want you to tell me what to do.

Here is an additional example of how you can ask for what you need:

> I want to share some issues that I am struggling with at work. I do not need you to provide a solution. What would feel nice is a hand on my shoulder, showing your support without judgment.

If you welcome his feedback, let him know:

> I am going to tell you about a situation at work that I am struggling with. I invite you to share your perspective and any advice on how I could better handle the situation.

When you are mainly looking for empathy, try saying this:

> Right now, I would appreciate some empathy from you. I realize that you may not understand how hard this (whatever the situation is) is for me because you do it so effortlessly, but please empathize and show me some kindness because I am struggling.

It is unreasonable and unrealistic to expect him to provide you his undivided attention every time you talk.[21] That's why it is essential to take the time to let him know when a situation warrants him to provide you with his focused attention. I know it would feel better if he instantly knew what you needed without you having to ask, but not speaking up and hoping for him to know magically is another mistake (one that is addressed later in this book).

He May Need Help Understanding Why Venting Is Beneficial

Are you someone that enjoys a good bout of venting? Through the act of verbalizing your problems, do you feel a little lighter as you verbally release tension and stress? Since many men typically do not talk about a problem unless they seek a solution, your guy may not be comfortable listening to you as you vent. You can alleviate the frustration of him trying to "fix" your problem by helping him understand that he does not need to provide a solution to the things you are venting about and that by just listening, he is helping.

If venting is not something he is in the habit of doing, he may have difficulty comprehending how simply listening to you vent can be helpful. Likewise, he may not understand that when you are upset, confused, or out of balance, you may need to find your way back to being centered. Explain to him that as he is attentively listening and being a sounding board while you are venting, it gives you a chance to gain awareness of the situation you are dealing with and helps you discover your own path back to being centered.[25]

You can help him see how his attentive listening benefits you by pausing after venting for a short time and offering a comment like this:

> Just after this little bit of venting, I am starting to feel better. Thank you for continuing to listen.

When you finish venting, here are some more things you can say to let him know you appreciate him for listening while also encouraging him to provide additional support in this manner:

- I am so glad I could get all this off my chest. Thanks for listening.
- You have no idea how much better I feel just by talking that out. I appreciate you for listening.
- Now that I had a chance to talk about it, I feel so much better. Thanks!
- I feel lighter since I was able to release all those feelings. Thanks for being there so I could talk that through.

Since the goal here is to feel heard, never miss an opportunity to express your appreciation to him when he is doing a good job silently paying attention because he may not realize how much you treasure feeling heard.

As women, we innately know how valuable it is to offer a listening ear. If you assume he should know how important it is for you to feel heard, you have forgotten he is not your girlfriend. You may have fallen into the mistake of not appreciating his differences. Remember that many men have a hard time listening to problems unless they can actively solve your problem. Slowly but surely, each time you express your gratitude for him listening, your approval helps him change his belief that he is not offering anything significant by staying quiet. Instead, he realizes that he is participating in a meaningful way by simply listening.

Please be mindful that the average guy does not have an unlimited attention span to listen to endless venting. Therefore, please keep your venting sessions to no longer than 10-15 minutes (which will feel like an eternity to most men). Try letting him know upfront how many minutes of venting time you'll need - this will increase the odds of him staying focused on what you are saying. Also, if you know your matter will require more than 15 minutes, please reach out to a girlfriend instead. Doing so can save your relationship from unnecessary wear and tear.

Your Questions May Mislead Him

After you have set the stage for what you want from him in a conversation, it is helpful to be aware of whether you ask rhetorical questions as you are processing your thoughts out loud.

For example, say you have just asked him just to listen as you vent about your frustrations with your sister, and a minute later, you say, "Why do you think my sister does that?" or "What am I supposed to do now?" Upon hearing either of those questions, he will probably assume you changed your mind and are now asking for his feedback. If you are like many women and regularly ask rhetorical questions, you could help avoid causing him confusion by providing a disclaimer.

Tell him that unless you have specifically asked for his feedback, for him to ignore your questions as you are just trying to make a point rather than seeking an answer from him. As someone likely to take your conversation literally, he will appreciate receiving this clarification in advance.

Windows and Women's Brains

I want to end this chapter by sharing something I stumbled upon while doing research for this book. I came across a blog on Shaunti Feldhahn's website where she shares a brilliant tip from the book *For Men Only*, written by her and her husband, Jeff. Many men have expressed gratitude to the authors for sharing this information that helped them understand the female brain, and I thought it would be beneficial to share it with you. Their observation about a woman's brain will probably not be a revelation to you, but it may be newsworthy to realize that most men are unaware of this.

If you are comparable to 80% of women, your brain wiring is similar to a computer desktop with multiple windows open at once.[26] Shaunti likens each window to a thought, feeling, worry, or problem you are pondering, and she describes how effortlessly you can switch between these windows, giving each one considerable attention at the same time. I had to laugh as I read this because right now, my desktop has 15 windows open, and I have been bouncing back and forth between them for hours. Thus, I can fully relate to what Shaunti is describing because my desktop at this moment is remarkably reflective of how my brain works.

According to Feldhahn, when a new thought or worry surfaces when a man is already dealing with one problem, most men can simply "close out" the bothersome window to remain focused on the original problem that has their attention.[26] On the other hand, the option of closing out a window that is bothering us is not available for most women. Men have no idea that our brains do not work like theirs, so in response to hearing us complain about something, they will often respond with "Just don't think about it," which is another way of saying, "Just close the window." It makes perfect sense to them. They are utterly unaware of how infuriating that comment can be. If you do not understand how his brain works, you may falsely perceive him as uncaring and purposely discounting your concerns and feelings. The truth is, when he says this, he IS considering your feelings and trying to be caring by sharing with you what works for him.

If you are like most women, you cannot just decide not to think about what is bothering you, but he has no idea because this comes naturally to him. When you can't stop thinking about a problem, you probably need to do something to resolve what is bothering you before letting it go. If you relate to this, it would be worth your time to explain this to the man in your life so he can better support you. I promise you he has no idea how to assist you appropriately and is doing the best he can from what he knows. Begin by sharing the analogy about open windows and how your brain works very differently from his. Next, ask him not to tell you, "Just don't think about it" or any variation of that. Ask him to say something like this instead:

> Are you struggling with an open window that you can't close? I'm sorry you're dealing with that. Is there something I can do that would help you feel better?[26(Item3)]

Now you are free to take action and deal with what's on your mind because, as women, we generally know what we need to do next. For example, maybe you want to reach out to a friend who has dealt with a similar situation to get her advice. Or perhaps you need to send an email to seek closure or gather further information. Or you may decide to work out and burn some energy before deciding what to do next. Or maybe your brain cannot make the next move until you have something to eat. Let him know that once you have decided what you need to do, you would like him to encourage you in your decision. If you need his help, now is the time to ask for it directly. For instance, you may ask him to get you some food or to watch the kids so you can work out.

I shared this insightful analogy authored by Shaunti Feldhahn because it provides another example of how quickly arguments and hurt feelings arise when we don't understand the differences and take them into account before passing judgment.

Mistake #6 – Top Takeaway Tips

♥ Set your conversation up for success

♥ Timing is everything

♥ Begin with the end in mind

Mistake #7

A Mistake That Leads to Defensiveness

It is always a mistake to word vomit when you are upset. When you are hurt or angry, that is the time you want to feel heard the most, but it is also the time you are most likely to choose words that will immediately put him on the defense and destroy any chance of being heard.

In this chapter, I want to highlight certain words that are problematic when trying to be heard. Using these words is a mistake because they set up your guy to be defensive when your genuine desire is for him to be responsive.

Sue Shepard, MFT

Never Use *Never* and Always Avoid *Always*

Never begin a conversation with "You never . . ." or "You always . . ." when trying to get your point across to him. It is a mistake because it immediately puts him on the defense. Not only will he miss the actual message you are trying to say, but he will surely come back instantly with the exception to what you said.

Never and *always* are absolutes, and they are problematic because they exaggerate the facts. These two words are guaranteed to derail your conversation as soon as you speak them. Since most men are concerned with accuracy, this will put your guy on the defense the minute he detects inaccuracy in the data. Then, the focus moves away from your primary concern, and a fight begins about the inaccurate details. You can avoid this pitfall by eliminating all absolutes.

Even if it's not your intent, these words feel demeaning to him because they dismiss previous attempts he has made. As soon as you use one of these words, instead of having the discussion you were hoping for, you may find yourself looking into the eyes of an angry person. The implications of your words insinuate that he is either lazy, thoughtless, or selfish (or all three).[27] He will battle against these disparaging inferences, and you lose any chance at a productive conversation.

Absolutes also have the power to bring your communication to a halt. For example, he may have gotten tired of numerous previous exaggerated accusations and upon hearing "You always" or "You never," he stops listening. He perceives nothing valid is coming, so he doesn't see the point in listening further.

You have probably heard before that *always* and *never* are problematic words in a relationship. Even so, I am addressing it again here at the risk of redundancy because this is a pitfall that I see women fall into regularly.

On many occasions, I do not think the woman is even aware she has used an absolute until I point it out. She is not expecting him to take the word literally and is primarily using the word as a way of expressing her frustration. She is not trying to be factual; she is expressing her feelings. Unfortunately, he completely misses her feelings because he is concerned with getting the facts right.

The pattern is the same; she starts a sentence with, "You never . . ." and he immediately feels wrongly accused in front of me, so he gets defensive and starts to prove to me why what she said is not accurate.

Here is an example:

> Her: You never bring me flowers.

Him: That's not true! I bought her flowers on her birthday last year.

I usually stop the discussion right there and point out her use of *never* and how it triggered his defensive response. It is at this moment in the conversation that most couples prepare for battle and choose opposing teams. To get them back on the same side of the concern, I encourage her to communicate what she wants rather than tell him what he is not doing. For example, I tell her that receiving flowers might not have the same meaning to him and ask her to describe why receiving flowers is so important to her and how she feels when he does bring her flowers.

The use of "You never . . ." and "You always . . ." are poison to your communication because they kill any chance of you feeling heard. For the health of your relationship, please remove these lethal words from your conversations.

How to Avoid Saying *Always*

If you tell a man, "You're always late!" the chances of you getting him to hear you and changing his behavior are slim to none. He will probably first tell you the exact date when he was on time that month. But more importantly, he cannot hear you because you did not honestly tell him what you wanted him to hear. You have valid reasons why you are upset when he is continuously late. Here are some alternative things you could say:

> I feel scared when I have to keep waiting. I worry something terrible has happened.
>
> I feel angry when I have to keep waiting. I hate being late to important events.
>
> I get worried when I have to keep waiting, and I do not know why you're late. I would rather use that time to get other things done instead of being so distressed.

In each of these responses, the focus is on your feelings while he remains out of it. Addressing your feelings rather than pointing the finger at him will reduce the chance of him becoming defensive.

Do not stop there. Follow up with an offer of negotiation. Say something like, "What do you think we can do so we are both happy?" This question will be music to his ears. Instead of creating a fight, you are seeking to reach a decision or agreement. You stayed true to yourself and communicated your feelings in a manner that he could hear you because he did not get triggered to go on the defense.

The Use of *But* Can Derail Your Entire Conversation

Most of us have a common reaction when we hear the word *but*. We instinctively know that the heart of the conversation is coming up. We usually tune out what was said first and listen carefully to what is coming next because we believe that part of the message will reflect what the person truly thinks or feels. You could share something meaningful with your guy and provoke an undesirable response simply by using this three-letter word.

But is used to join two phrases in one sentence; however, it basically diminishes the first phrase entirely. By understanding how this little word can derail your whole conversation, you can make a simple word swap and get your communication back on track. *And* can join the exact two phrases without dismissing the preceding phrase. For example, consider the following two remarks with only one word changed:

> I know you had a long day, **but** I still need your help.

> I know you had a long day, **and** I still need your help.

In the first one, he could feel that your need completely overrides his hard day. Then due to resentment, he may ignore your request for help. In the second one, he can hear your acknowledgment of his exhausting day and consequently, he will be more open to you seeking his assistance.

The use of *but* can also undo praise. Think about how differently he might interpret these two statements:

> I really appreciated your help today, **but** . . .
>
> I really appreciated your help today, **and** . . .

In the first one, he will immediately think you are about to say something negative and will focus on what he potentially screwed up and not even hear your compliment. In the second statement, he has no idea what you will say next, but he does know that you valued his help today. By using *and*, he can feel affirmed by the first part of the sentence regardless of what comes next.

Another reason to avoid using the word *but* is because it can invalidate his opinion. Whether you mean to or not, when you say *but*, you can be perceived as defensive and unwilling to hear what he has to say. He could easily interpret your *but* as you discounting or negating what he is trying to tell you.

For example, say you are talking to your guy, he shares his point of view, and then your reply begins with *but*. Before you even complete your thought, he will conclude that you disagree with him. He might think every word that follows your *but* is you telling him why he's wrong, so he may stop listening before you can finish your comment.

Without meaning to, your conversation can turn adversarial. Starting your sentence with *but* could immediately put him on the defense and position you two as opponents ready for battle. In replying to his opinion, try saying "Yes, and . . ." Doing so will keep him engaged in the exchange rather than shutting him down. Starting your response with "Yes, and . . ." allows the conversation to expand rather than canceling out what he said and prevents it from turning into a fight.

But Can Be Used Favorably

Arguably, it is best to avoid using *but* when it follows a positive statement so that anything good you want to communicate does not get negated entirely. As we have seen, not only can it remove the significance of the positive statement, but it can also leave the impression that the opposite is true. Surprisingly, *but* can be used favorably. Consider changing the order of your remark by putting the negative part at the beginning:

If you said to him:

> I see your point of view, but I disagree.

He would hear this instead:

> She does not agree, and she probably does not even see my point of view.

Consider saying this instead:

> I disagree, but I do see your point of view.

Can you feel the shift of impact? By putting the negative portion of the sentence before the *but*, it tones it down and gives more significance to the positive statement that follows.

When It Is Appropriate to Banish *But* Altogether

Sometimes it is best to banish *but* altogether. Test out removing *but* to eliminate any confusion and to ward off any defensiveness.

If you said to him:

> I like the color you picked out for the family room, but I think it's too dark.

He would hear this instead:

> She thinks it's too dark and she probably doesn't even like the color.

Consider saying this instead:

> I like the color you picked out for the family room. I think it's too dark.

Now he can hear that you are pleased with the color he chose, and he is open to hearing that maybe the lack of natural light in the room requires a brighter color.

The many examples shared above illustrate why saying *but* can be problematic when seeking to feel heard. Hopefully, you will be more conscious of your use of *but* and will be able to quickly identify when it is responsible for derailing your conversation.

Reconsider Starting Your Sentences with *Let's*

Do you ever start your sentences with *Let's*? For example, "Let's stop by the grocery store on the way home," or "Let's have Chinese food for dinner tonight." Have you ever felt pushback or even anger from your guy when you do this?

If so, let me explain what is happening. You may find this a total mystery, like I did, because when I use *Let's*, I am just making a recommendation, not making a demand. From my perspective, if he does not want to do whatever I am suggesting, he can simply offer an alternative. Instead, I have learned that he feels anger when I say this because he thinks I am ordering him around and telling him what to do. This notion completely caught me off guard because I made a polite suggestion and was open to him offering another option.

In doing some research to understand why he reacted so strongly to what I considered a simple suggestion, I learned from Tannen that the misunderstanding of the word *Let's* can be traced back to conversational styles used by girls and boys when they play. Little girls were observed as young as ages two to five using *Let's* to propose what action they would take during their playtime. The girls were careful to use words that would influence one another without telling them what to do.[5]

Boys, on the other hand, freely issued commands to one another. Within their conversational style, boys and men are accustomed to telling each other what to do, and they retain their status by being resistant.

That is why the act of you politely suggesting something without being confrontational gets perceived as you trying to get your way by being manipulative. He feels that you are trying to control him, and out of anger, he adamantly opposes anything you suggest. His reaction is contrary to your intention, so you may find it challenging to understand where he is coming from.

Not all men have an aversion to the use of *Let's*. However, if you have observed it being problematic in your relationship, you may want to reconsider using *Let's* and utilize a more straightforward approach when making requests.

Keep the Door Closed on Exit Threats

An exit threat is when you exclaim during an argument that you want to break up or you want a divorce. It is only a threat and not something you are ready to act on. For simplicity, I have focused on the word *divorce* in the context of marriage in this section. However, the concepts I share will also pertain to unmarried relationships because all exit threats are equally damaging.

I want to differentiate between thoughts of divorce and actual threats. If you just have an occasional thought about divorce without verbalizing it, that is surprisingly common. The National Divorce Decision-Making Project did a national survey with 3,000 people who had been married for at least one year and ranged in age from 25 to 50. The findings revealed that more than half of the individuals had thoughts of divorce.[28] The good news is that 90% of them did not take action to pursue a divorce. Instead, the majority of them put effort into working on their marriage. The thought by itself is not harmful. It is when that thought turns into a verbal attack that it becomes dangerous.

You chose this book because you do not feel heard in your relationship. That is painful. If this has continued for any length of time, your pain has intensified. Consequently, you can be easily triggered during an argument when you don't feel heard. From a place of deep pain, you may lash out in anger and threaten your husband with divorce. Since you are reading this book to improve your communication, your actions show you are still trying to make your relationship better and probably aren't at the point of pursuing a divorce. See if any of the reasons below describe why you may have resorted to issuing a threat of divorce.

Reasons you may threaten divorce[29]:

- You may be trying to get his attention. You may feel that you have talked and talked, and he never seems to listen. So, you try throwing divorce into the conversation to get him to pay attention.

- It may be an attempt to get him to understand how frustrated and hopeless you feel. On the other hand, you may have tried multiple times to express your feelings and still feel unheard, so you have descended to issuing a threat.

- You may try to hurt him so he can feel how much pain you are in. You lash out from a place of pain, hoping he can finally grasp how awful you feel.

- You may feel insecure in the permanence of your marriage and take the first strike from a defensive posture, hoping for reassurance.

All the reasons described above show that you are hoping for change in your relationship. You are seeking:

- His attention
- His understanding
- His empathy
- His reassurance

Unfortunately, threatening divorce is probably the single most hurtful thing you can say to him - especially if it was a tactic to get him to be more present in the relationship. The threat of abandonment can shut him down in a profound way because what he hears is, "I am leaving and I do not love you anymore."[30] The result of an exit threat is rarely the outcome you were seeking. Instead, the threat destroys trust and inflicts injury to the core of his being. You risk causing damage that is incapable of being repaired.

If you have previously thrown out the word *divorce* during a fight, please commit never to repeat it (unless you have resolved to end your marriage). You want communication to improve. That requires trust in each other. If your husband is living under a threat of divorce, he may avoid any conversation that feels like it may lead to an argument.

To seek the trust, love, and closeness you desire from your husband will involve you becoming vulnerable and setting your anger aside. I know it is hard to be vulnerable when you are upset, so take time to calm down so you can explain to him what the real hurt is underneath your anger. For example, try saying something like this:

> I feel very alone in this marriage. I am in pain because I do not feel heard when I try to talk to you. This troubling pattern has been happening for a while, and I am feeling very discouraged. If

we can't resolve this, it scares me that we will never have the closeness I truly desire to have with you. I want to learn from what hasn't worked to move forward together and discover ways to make it work.

Changing your past patterns involves strengthening your commitment – which is the direct opposite of issuing an exit threat. The remarks above guide you to be vulnerable and express your feelings while also reassuring him of your desire to maintain a close relationship.

Tip on How to Seek His Input Without Asking a Question (to avoid putting him on the defense)

Since this chapter is about a mistake that leads to defensiveness, this tip will help avoid putting him on the defense.

When you ask a question like, "What are you going to do about your brother getting so drunk at our house?" be prepared for him to become defensive. You increase the probability of being heard and obtaining his input if you avoid questions like this. That kind of question will often instigate an argument because he may perceive it as a power challenge. If so, it will result in him becoming irritable, frustrated, and defensive – all barriers to you feeling heard.

You can eliminate the power struggle and elicit his response by saying this instead, "I wonder how we can address your brother if he starts to get super drunk at our next party?"

Can you feel the shift in energy from the initial question versus this statement? Instead of judgment and demands, this statement presents a problem for him to solve (and we know how much he likes to solve problems). It allows him to come alongside you instead of him feeling attacked by you.

Instead of asking questions that might put him on the defense, try using sentences that start with:

"I wonder how we can . . ."

"It would be good to know . . ."

"I would feel so much better if we found a way through . . ."

"It sure would help alleviate stress for me if we found a solution to. . ."

By utilizing these sentences instead of asking questions that he might perceive as judgmental and demanding, you will have prevented much unnecessary defensiveness. Consequently, since he won't feel attacked by your words, he will lower his defenses, and you can feel heard.

Mistake #7 – Top Takeaway Tips

♥ Absolutely avoid using absolutes

♥ To reduce defensiveness, don't start a sentence with *But*

♥ Keep the door closed on exit threats

WHAT'S YOUR COMMUNICATION STYLE?

In the next chapter, Mistake #8 will be focusing on what style of communication you engage in when talking to your husband or your boyfriend.

In just a minute, you can discover whether you use a direct or indirect style to communicate in your relationship. Take this quick 10 question quiz and it will reveal your communication style.

To take the Quiz,
just scan this QR code with your phone

Or visit bit.ly/quiz-learn-style

Mistake #8

A Mistake That Leads to Your Needs Not Being Met

It is a mistake to believe that he should anticipate your wants and needs without you expressing them. Essentially, this is expecting him to be able to read your mind.

He Should Know...

I encounter this mistake frequently when a couple comes in for marriage counseling. The woman will state with absolute certainty that she feels she should not have to tell him what she needs and that he should know. An example would be, "Why should I have to ask him to help me with the kids? Why can't he see how tired I am and just jump in?"

If he were a woman, this would be a reasonable expectation since women often intuitively feel the needs of others and are quick to extend themselves when a need arises. We were raised in a culture where anticipating needs and lovingly offering to help is welcomed and desired. However, it is a mistake to expect a man to operate in the same manner. In the culture he grew up in, the expectation was if you want help, you need to ask for it. Most men do not have the built-in antennae that many women have that would signal him to survey a situation or read a person to see if he needs to offer his support. Many things simply are not on his radar because, from his frame of reference, he naturally concludes that you will speak up if you need assistance.

Bearing that in mind, keep yourself from jumping to the conclusion that he is aware of your need and has decided not to help. Instead, please give him the benefit of the doubt. It could be that he simply does not see it or is waiting for you to ask for his help. Being raised in a male culture of self-sufficiency, he may perceive it rude to offer assistance without being asked first.[1] Once you grasp that his actions result from how men operate differently, you will understand it is not reflective of his love for you.

The happiest couples I have in my office are the ones that choose to believe that their partner's heart is in the right place and that their intentions are good. If you start with this premise, it will come from a place of trust when you ask for his assistance. He can hear you better if you come from a place of believing the best in him than if you assume he did not want to help you in the first place.

If He Loved Me...

Occasionally women take it a step further and exclaim, "If he loved me, then he would know that I need help." That is a dangerous assumption because it concludes that he must not love her since he failed to offer his assistance. It is simply not true, and it leads to much resentment.

When I hear this inaccurate conclusion expressed in my office, I address it immediately because it can damage a relationship as time goes on. For example, suppose a woman believes a man's love is determined by whether he is capable of "knowing" what she wants without expressing it directly. In that case, the relationship is doomed for failure because he will never live up to this expectation.

Hasn't there been a time when you do not even know what you want? Or what you want at 10:00 a.m. is not the same as what you want at 5:00 p.m.? You may want something specific on Tuesday, but he will completely miss the mark and have no idea why if he shows up with that on Thursday. When you require him to anticipate your needs without taking it upon yourself to make your needs known, it sets him up for failure, ultimately resulting in your needs not being met.

Some women in my office will push back and say, "If I have to tell him what I want, then he'll only be doing it because I told him, and it won't matter then." Unfortunately, you put him in a no-win situation with that kind of thinking. He cannot meet your need if he has no idea what you want. A more optimistic way to assess his actions would be to realize that if he does what you ask for, it undoubtedly shows that he is doing it because he cares about you. He clearly is not choosing to do it because it is of consequence to him. His action to respond to your request must be received and internalized as a caring and loving act. He is choosing YOU over something else he would rather be doing. If you devalue his effort because you had to verbalize your need, you have again set him up for failure. His willingness to stop doing what he was doing and start doing what you want him to do positively says, "I care." If he does something for you outside his ordinary routine, he chooses to do it because you matter to him.

Appreciate his willingness to meet your need, even if it does not come naturally to him. His inability to anticipate your needs is not a measure of his love or a defect in him. Instead, view this as simply one of the ways you two differ. Just because it may seem obvious to you does not mean it will instinctively occur to him.

Direct Versus Indirect Communication

When indirect communication is taking place, the speaker's true intention is not apparent. It may not be evident because the speaker is talking around the subject. Or it is hidden because the speaker is trying to convey something with non-verbal clues such as tone of voice, facial expressions, hand gestures or other body language. When someone uses an indirect communication style, the listener is held responsible for correctly interpreting what the speaker is trying to express.

Conversely, when direct communication happens, the true intentions of the speaker are transparent and unmistakable. There is no need for the listener to decipher the message because it is spoken clearly and straightforward.

Here is an example of the two communication styles in use:

Indirect communication:	What's that awful smell? It's coming from the kitchen trash can because it is so full that the lid won't stay closed.

Direct communication: Will you please take out the trash.

Do you ever drop a hint or give indirect clues to what you want or need? You can quickly begin to harbor resentment because he is not picking up on the clues you are leaving. Since most men's communication style is rather direct and blunt, he may not be in the habit of looking for clues and hints while you are talking to him. Honestly, your ability to speak directly, which is a language he is fluent in, is superior to his ability to understand your indirect language. He may pick up on your indirect message once in a blue moon, but do you really want to leave it to chance? Since the goal here is to be heard, it is worth your effort to retrain yourself to use a more direct communication style so you are both using a common language. Doing so provides a greater chance of being heard because this is a language he can recognize and comprehend.

If you ask him, I bet he would say that he wishes you were more open about what you honestly want and more direct about what you genuinely do not like. The most effective thing you can do to bring about a greater chance of being heard is directly asking for what you want.

If you are an indirect communicator, you may not be conveying what you want with just your words and may be sending messages via your long pauses, silence or tone of voice.[31] If your guy is a direct communicator, most likely, he will fail to pick up on the nuances and subtleties of your indirect communication. He may have no idea what he is missing. That will leave him frustrated because he will know you're upset but be unable to figure out what he's doing wrong.

It is noteworthy to mention that many women prefer indirect communication as a way to avoid conflict, disharmony, and making situations uncomfortable.[31] Unfortunately, when you leave him responsible for correctly interpreting your subtle message, you've actually increased the likelihood of conflict. You not getting your needs met will lead to resentment and unhappiness. His not knowing what he did (or didn't) do to make you upset will lead to anger and frustration. These reactions will wreak havoc on your relationship and leave you both feeling misunderstood.

Consider these three examples:

1. When we have a baby, it would be nice to have family support.
2. I can't imagine having a baby without the help of my family.
3. Before we have a baby, I want to move closer to my family.

Example #1 is just a statement. It does not convey a want or need. He could quickly agree with you and have no idea that you want something from him.

Example #2 is less vague, but it still does not directly tell him what you are hoping for.

Example #3 is a clear example of what direct communication looks like. It is easy to see why this example leaves less risk for misunderstanding and a greater chance of addressing your need.

Avoid Indirect Words *Can* & *Could,* and Choose Direct Words *Will* & *Would*

Many women will make requests using the following C words: *Could you* or *Can you.* Typically, women choose these words because they come across as more polite.[1] While conversing with other women, the C words are used regularly without opposition. For example, if you said to another woman, "Can you take me off speakerphone? I'm having a hard time hearing you," she would interpret this as a polite request and would readily respond without resistance.

Unfortunately, many men have an aversion to hearing the words *Could you* or *Can you.* They categorize these C words as indirect and weak, so they don't trust them.[1] Men are more responsive to the following W words: *Would you* or *Will you.* If you said to a man, "Can you bring in the trash cans?" he may feel insulted because, of course, he *can* bring in the trash cans. "Will you bring in the trash cans" communicates a request to him. *Can you* may be interpreted as an insult that could result in undesirable behavior like:

- Him becoming irritated
- Him begrudgingly completing the task while storing up resentment
- Him choosing to ignore your request altogether

Since you don't have an aversion to the C words, it may be difficult to understand why it matters to him. Let me put it into perspective so you'll have an idea of where your guy is coming from. Let's say on the day your guy decides to propose to you, he gets down on one knee and says, "Could you marry me?"[1] Those words sound weak and like he is questioning whether he is worthy of your love. Instead of being romantic, you are turned off by his insecurity and low self-esteem. Now imagine him getting down on one knee and saying, "Would you marry me?" Right away, your heart responds to his strength and vulnerability. Do you see how the change in one letter has the power to communicate a completely different message? I hope this allows you to better understand why your guy may be turned off by these C words (*could* & *can*) and inspires you to be willing to replace them with the W words (*would* & *will*).

Three Indirect Words to Eliminate from Your Vocabulary

Have you ever participated in a dialogue similar to this?

    Him: Is there something wrong?

    Her: No.

    Him: You seem upset. What's going on?

    Her: Nothing.

    Him: If you say so.

    Her: Whatever.

    Him: I thought you said it was nothing.

    Her: Fine.

In this example, she initially displays some non-verbal indication of being upset, hoping he will tune in. He then asks her a direct question hoping to find out what she isn't saying. However, rather than meet his direct inquiries with a direct response, she continues to supply indirect answers that leave them both feeling frustrated and disconnected.

If you can relate to this, I encourage you to ban these words from all conversations with your guy: *nothing, whatever,* and *fine.*

These indirect words will never help you reach your goal of feeling heard. To achieve that goal will require you to express yourself more honestly and openly. When you communicate clearly and directly, it will cultivate connection instead of disconnection.

Do You Expect Him to Read Your Mind?

If you are more comfortable using indirect communication, you may ask, "Why do I have to be so straightforward?" You may wish he could just figure out there is a problem and take action to correct it. Regrettably, this is a fantasy that will never become a reality because he is not a mind reader.

Now is the time to stop blaming him for not meeting the needs that you have never directly communicated to him. For example, say you've been feeling a little disconnected because you haven't been spending enough time together, so you set plans for the two of you to spend Saturday together. Then the night before, his brother gets last-minute tickets to the game on Saturday. He says, "I know we were planning to spend the day together, but these tickets are too good to pass up. Would it bother you if I went to the game?" You respond, "Of course, you should go," but you deliver your response with your arms crossed and while looking down. You indicated your disapproval using nonverbal clues.

You may believe you sent him a clear message that you were not okay with him going and feel he disregarded your feelings. On the other hand, he is sure that you verbalized a direct message indicating that he should go, so he will be unprepared for the fight that will undoubtedly occur after he returns from the game. You expected him to know that you didn't really want him to go, but he missed the subtle clues and just heard your comment granting your approval. Men have a hard enough time figuring out what you mean when you do use your words – they absolutely suck at mind reading.

It bears repeating, men do not think like us. When you rely on someone so fundamentally different from you to decipher what you're saying without directly stating it, you will end up disappointed.

Dropping Hints Leads to Disappointment

Men will often sit in my office and express their frustration with women failing to just say what they want. These are men that want to please their partners, but they can't get it right because they keep missing the hints. If he wants to make you happy, make it easy for him. Avoid dropping hints and tell him directly what you want.

Say there is a new restaurant that you are looking forward to trying. You start by dropping these hints over a couple of weeks:

> "There is a new sushi bar opening up in town."
>
> "My parents went to the new sushi bar and said it was delicious."
>
> "The local food critic just did a review on the new sushi bar and he gave it five stars."

After a while, you're frustrated because he hasn't made a reservation yet. What you may not understand is that all these statements are just conveying information. None of them state a request. The only way to ensure that he knows you want to go there is to tell him directly. Try saying this instead:

> "There is a new sushi bar in town that I've heard great things about. I would love to go this weekend."

The same principle applies to dropping hints for a gift you would like. If you show your guy a picture on Instagram and say, "Look what Jennifer got as a gift. Isn't that stunning?" he may agree with you but have no idea you would want one too because you never actually said that. A more direct way to convey your true intent would be to add the following: "If you are looking for a gift idea for my birthday, I would love to have one of these. I'll send you the link."

If receiving gifts on your birthday or holidays is important, and you've been disappointed in the past with what he has or hasn't done, try being more direct with your expectations. He may be trying to please you and is just as frustrated with not being able to make you happy. Determine a successful outcome for both of you by providing precise details of what you want. To make this work, you'll have to let go of any belief that says, "If I have to tell him what I want, it will take all the romance out of it." Look at it from this perspective, how romantic does the night turn out when you're disappointed with the gift you received, and he feels bad for letting you down?

A girlfriend of mine used to go to the local mall and take pictures of the things she wanted and send them to her husband with the exact location in the store where he could find them. Nowadays, we can purchase almost anything online. You can easily locate what you'd like and send him the links. Be sure to include any specifics like size, color, etc. so you don't end up with the right item in the wrong size or the correct size in the wrong color.

The problem with giving a man a hint and hoping he will figure out what is really on your mind is that, in the beginning, he will go into problem-solving mode and do his best to figure out what you are trying to communicate. But if he does not have enough information, he will inevitably get it wrong. Then after multiple times of letting you down and facing your disappointment, he will stop trying because his attempts at trying to decipher your clues have been unsuccessful, and he deems any future effort as futile.

By communicating very clearly and removing all the guesswork, you set him up for success. He feels good because he can make you happy, and you win because the gift you unwrap is precisely the gift you desired.

Only Say "I Don't Care" if You Genuinely DON'T Care

Selecting a place to eat is often a point of contention for many couples. I see this pattern repeatedly when a woman uses indirect language to appear flexible and not too picky about where she is open to dining when that's not even close to being the truth.

For example, if he asks you where you want to go for dinner, don't say "I don't care" unless you genuinely DON'T care. Guys hate when you say you don't care, and then they suggest a place, and you turn it down.[32] If you really didn't care, you would be okay with any suggestion he made. Saying, "I don't care," falsely communicates that you will have a meal anywhere when the truth is there are places you are unwilling to eat. As luck will have it, those will be the exact places he will propose. Each time you reject one of his recommendations, you risk him getting frustrated or building resentment towards you. Over time, he may fail to offer any suggestions because he believes you will ultimately override them.

When you have a preference, simply state it. If you are open to suggestions, ask him to name three places he would like to eat at, and you'll pick one. If there is something you are not willing to eat, let him know. For example, "I had Chinese for lunch, so anything but that." If there are one or more places that he favors that you know you don't feel like eating at, indicate that you are open to anything except: name the particular place(s). If you truly don't know what you feel like eating, you can say, "I can't decide what I feel like eating. Please throw out some suggestions. I'll let you know what sounds good." Remember, "I don't know" and "I don't care" communicate very different messages. Be precise with your words to avoid conflict.

Silence Is Not Always Golden

Another indirect approach utilized by some women is the "cold shoulder," where you ignore him or refuse to speak to him unless necessary. Instead of telling him directly, you use silence to convey something is wrong without telling him why.

Some women take it too far and stop talking altogether for days on end. Often when they end up in my office after one of these prolonged silent periods, the men will say they have no idea why she is so upset. It will take most of the session to unravel her pain and get to the heart of the matter, where she can thoroughly explain what hurt her and lead to the silence. Too often, I see the men discover what exactly is upsetting her for the *first* time. She mistakenly believed that she could simply go quiet, and it would give him time to realize what he did wrong and make it right.

In addition, she sometimes has used the silence to punish him for whatever offense he has done. Unfortunately, the punishment will never lead to reform if he has no idea what he did wrong in the first place. The truth is that the only way he will understand what he did to upset you, is to tell him directly.

Men Are Less Likely to Pick Up Some Non-verbal Clues

Research has concluded, and studies show, that women are better at recognizing emotions from faces than men and that women are faster than men in reading facial emotions in general.[33]

Since this comes more naturally to women, it is understandable why you may mistakenly expect him to pick up on your unhappiness through non-verbal cues. Think about the last time you met with one of your close friends and she showed up sad; you probably knew before she even opened her mouth that something was wrong. Because we have grown accustomed to our close friends picking up when something is wrong with us, you may naturally feel that the man that loves you should be able to do the same. Unfortunately, the wiring in his brain is not the same as yours. As a result, he is at a significant disadvantage when it comes to facial emotion recognition. Instead of holding it against him that he is not observant, tell him what you feel and need. It could be, "I feel sad right now and would like a hug" or "I feel sad and need time to process it. I do not want to be touched at this moment."

Asking for What You Want Versus Demanding

When I encourage you to ask for what you want, there is no room for these obvious ways of coming across as demanding: complaining, yelling, pouting, nagging, making snide remarks, or having a meltdown to get heard. However, you may not realize that when you ask nicely, but he does not have the option of saying *no* without you getting upset, you are still being demanding.

It becomes a demand the minute you fail to accept his *no* without reacting negatively. For example, say you ask him to get the holiday decorations down before he goes to bed because you want to start decorating the house in the morning. Then he replies, "I'm really beat tonight. I'll get them first thing in the morning." At this point, it's still 50/50 whether this is a request or a demand.

If you respond, "That would be wonderful. I want to start decorating first thing tomorrow," that is undeniably a request. On the other hand, if you get upset and reply, "I can't believe you can't take a couple of minutes to do this for me now," then you are making a demand.

It's always acceptable to ask for what you want as long as you can handle hearing *no*. Your request becomes a demand when you insist that he give you what you want, and you become upset if he fails to do so.[34] Using direct communication to ask for support involves telling him what you want and need while remaining open to hearing his side. It also includes you engaging in a dialogue where you welcome his feedback and are receptive to making compromises.

Graciously Accept His "No"

Most of us are much more willing to say *yes* when we know our *no* will be received well, and your guy is no exception. However, if you haven't been in the practice of accepting his *no* without some fallout, then it's time to show him that he can say *no*, and you will graciously accept it.

Do you ever intuitively know that his response will be *no*, so you don't even bother asking? Often when that happens, you still feel the same rejection and hurt as if he said *no*, but he has no idea what caused the fallout because the entire transaction occurred in your head.[1]

When you quietly relinquish your needs and don't ask, how is he supposed to know how many times you needed him? By not speaking up, you have already accepted his no. It will serve you both better if you start asking for those things that you have already determined that he'll respond *no* to and practice being accepting and trusting. In doing so, each time you ask him for support and do not reject him, his trust in you will grow, and he'll be more responsive to your future requests.

The goal here is to make it safe for him to say *no*, so only choose a situation that you are comfortable with his response being *no*.

An example of this would be:

> You two usually go out to eat at a place you both enjoy and then head home afterward. You enjoy singing and have a passion for karaoke. However, you never ask him to go because you know he doesn't like to get up in front of people.

Since you can almost guarantee that he'll say *no*, say this to him at dinner:

> Would you like to stop at the Karaoke Lounge on the way home and do karaoke with me?

When he says no, be gracious and offer a genuine response of, "No problem."

He might be surprised that you asked him to go, but he will be shocked that you accepted his *no* without resistance. Try to find other situations where you can practice asking for something where you are genuinely okay with him saying no. Each time you graciously accept his *no*, he will remember that. Then, the next time you ask for his support lovingly and make it safe for him to refuse, he'll be more receptive to your request.

Final Thoughts

If you have ever tried putting together a jigsaw puzzle, you know the best strategy to solve it and see what you are working with is to start by laying out all the pieces face up. That is a similar strategy to use when making your needs known. Start by being clear about what you want and using direct communication to put all the relevant information out in plain view. If you dislike something, tell him explicitly. If you like something, let him know precisely what it is. If you want something, ask for it specifically. You leave no room for doubt or miscommunication when you communicate directly and avoid dropping hints or relying on non-verbal clues.

Staying aware of how different you two communicate is essential in building a stronger relationship. Never assume he automatically understands where you are coming from without you taking the time to tell him directly.

Mistake #8 – Top Takeaway Tips

- Indirect requests lead to miscommunication – ask directly
- Replace "Can you" with "Will you" & "Could you" with "Would you"
- You will get more *Yes's* when you graciously accept his *No's*

Mistake #9

A Mistake That Leads to Resentment

Forgetting to greet him is a mistake. The little things we forget to do can make all the difference in the world. There is significant value in offering a meaningful hello, goodbye, goodnight, good morning, etc. Life gets busy, and we forget to provide simple greetings – most of us do not even realize we have stopped doing it. Do not confuse *simple* with *unimportant*, because taking the time to extend these small gestures to him can do wonders for your relationship.

Small Gestures Can Affect the Health of Your Relationship

I am going to talk about the simple task of greeting your guy daily. This is something that you can start doing today. It will cost you nothing and will only occupy a handful of minutes each day. It's remarkable how much these simple daily practices can contribute to reduced conflict and increased connection.

The opposite is also true – the lack of offering these basic gestures may slowly erode the relationship. For example, it is possible that failing to greet your partner with a simple "good morning" or failing to thank him for small things, like taking the dog for a walk (even though it is something you expect him to do), may cause him to start to build resentment towards you. That resentment can result in him tuning you out, ultimately resulting in you not being heard.

Do Not Assume Greetings Don't Matter to Him

You may think that your guy is someone that does not care about simple greetings. If this is just an assumption that you have never actually clarified with him, I challenge you to keep an open mind.

I was doing therapy with a couple where the husband was one of the most emotionally detached individuals I had ever met. He was a very hard-working man and spent long hours at work, and when he was home, he would retreat to his home office and work long into the night with relatively little interaction with his wife. He readily admitted that he became self-sufficient at a young age and did not have emotional needs like his wife.

As a result, his wife assumed he placed little to no value on simple greetings and had stopped offering them over the years. So she was shocked when he shared in session how much he missed her poking her head into his home office to say goodbye when she was going out or good night when she was heading to bed. She had no idea these gestures meant so much to him and was happy to learn that she could offer something so small and he'd find it meaningful.

Show Him That He Matters in Your Life

It's easy to become so comfortable in a serious relationship that you forget to recognize your partner, the other half of your dynamic duo. That's why it is critical to take a moment every day to appreciate him in some way—even if it's just saying hello and goodbye when he arrives and leaves each day.

Gratitude is the willingness to show appreciation for someone or something. An easy way you can do that is through the use of small gestures. For example, kissing him hello and goodbye, expressing a meaningful good morning and good night, or just stopping what you are doing to acknowledge him as he walks through the door.

Each little gesture adds to something of the utmost importance: demonstrating to your partner that you genuinely care about his presence in your life. Conversely, if you discard such commonplace moments, you may inadvertently convey that he doesn't matter as much to you as you know he truly does.

You may be on the receiving end of not feeling that you matter as much to him anymore. The hope is that once you start acknowledging him as he comes and goes, he will respond in kind and eventually, it will be an equal exchange.

So the bottom line is to be intentional and give attention to the everyday greetings. Make them a reality. They are more crucial than you realize since they are daily proof that he's still the most important person in your life.

Have You Become Lax Over Time?

Think back to when you two first started dating. Remember when you missed him while you two were apart? How you looked forward with anticipation to seeing him again? Can you recall how you couldn't help but smile big because you were so excited to see him walk through the door finally? Your response was effortless because it flowed naturally from your delight in being with the person that mattered the most to you.

The enthusiasm you easily expressed at the beginning of your relationship most likely has declined over time. Typically, it's not because you dislike him or no longer appreciate him. Instead, it's likely because you have become too comfortable with one another.[35] You've grown accustomed to him walking through the door, so you probably take it for granted and no longer show him how much he means to you. If you are like most couples, you haven't stopped appreciating him as time has gone by. Instead, you have just stopped expressing that gratitude, which can result in him feeling taken for granted.

Be mindful to not let familiarity get in the way of you greeting him in a loving manner. Make a point of welcoming him even though time may have worn you down and you're out of practice. There is much to be said for showering him with affection the moment you see one another. It immediately eases tension and sets the stage for the rest of your time together.

The First Few Minutes With Your Guy Are Vital

The first couple minutes after you wake up together and those first minutes when you two meet at the end of the day play a vital role in the happiness and closeness of your relationship. It is during these encounters that you have a chance to rekindle your most gratifying feelings for one another. By being intentional with these greetings each day, you can convey that you care about him, that he is important to you, and that you welcome his presence in your life. Acknowledging him in this manner helps to develop a more loving, lasting bond.

The Value of a Warm "Welcome Home" Is Undeniable

What if I told you that the first minute or two when you greet him are vital to the health of your relationship? When you see him at the end of the day, the initial 60-120 seconds sets the tone for the rest of the night. So please make the most of it. Use that greeting to reconnect with him and show him how much you love him.

You have the ability to touch your guy's heart in a subtle way by simply adding warmth and enthusiasm to your greeting. You can be bold and spectacular if you have the time, but don't pass on an opportunity to extend a simple, heart-warming greeting even if you're busy.

When he walks through the door, stop what you are doing. Look him in the eyes. Demonstrate that you're willing to give him your undivided attention for at least a minute or two. Express to him how happy you are to have him home. Let him know how much you value his presence.

When verbalizing that you are delighted to see him, here are some examples of things you might say:

"Yay - you're here!"

"You've arrived!"

"Hooray – you're home!"

"Throughout the day, I've been looking forward to seeing you."

"You've been on my mind today. It's nice to see your face."

"I've been eagerly awaiting your arrival."

"So nice to have you home – I missed you."

By Lighting up When He Returns Home, You Ignite His Heart

You may be surprised at what eye contact and a smile that lights up your face can do for your relationship. It may seem insignificant, but the way you look at him and welcome him home can have a significant impact on how loved he feels and can set the tone for the remainder of the evening.

> "We shall never know all the good that a simple smile can do."[36]
> MOTHER TERESA

When he returns home, stop whatever you are doing for a moment, look up, make eye contact, and "light up."[37] When I say "light up," I am not referring to the typical social smile that we extend to everyone else. That smile involves just lifting the corners of your mouth. The smile that lights up your face is the one that reaches your eyes. A genuine smile, one that signifies your absolute pleasure, not only displays a mouth smile, but also leads to wrinkling around the eyes so that your eyes are smiling too.

Here is how you can offer him a smile that shows you're delighted he's there: take a moment to recall why you married him in the first place. Once you are in touch with that warm feeling, let it shape your smile, put a twinkle in your eyes, and light up your face. Your affection for him will shine from your face, and he will be able to see your love for him in your eyes.

Create a Greeting Ritual That Fits You

Perhaps you and your partner aren't as outgoing when it comes to showing affection. You are not obligated to jump into his arms (however, if you feel like it, go for it!). A tender kiss, a warm embrace, or a heartfelt smile may be part of your greeting ritual. Or it can be simply your eyes lighting up when you see him. It is not necessary for it to be complex or overly romantic.

The formula for the perfect greeting is momentarily giving him your full attention while expressing real excitement at seeing him. Make your routine fit your personality rather than utilizing predetermined acts or phrases that aren't suitable for you. Simply stop what you are doing, set aside unpleasant feelings from the day, and choose to greet him in a manner that conveys, "I'm delighted to see you, I missed you while you were away, and I'm glad you're home."

If you're having trouble in your marriage right now, still give this a shot. These seemingly insignificant changes can often offer your marriage a whole new perspective. Please don't give up if he doesn't notice immediately. Keep it up. Change takes time, but once you start changing the small things, the bigger ones have a way of taking care of themselves.

Being Distracted May Send an Unintentional Message

When he comes home and you remain distracted by other activities, it can incorrectly send him the message that you value whatever has your attention more than you value him.

Be strategic and express your greeting with purpose by giving him your undivided attention. He will undoubtedly feel the difference between a distracted greeting and one filled with warm-heartedness. While you are pre-occupied, a detached acknowledgment doesn't count as a proper greeting and tends to make things worse.

Say you have been apart and right when you see each other, you are inattentive, uninterested, preoccupied or in a solemn mood. Unfortunately, it will color the atmosphere and affect the quality of your interaction for the evening. A simple "Hi" without warmth or eye contact can change a potentially pleasant and comfortable evening into one that is quiet and distant.

What Not to Do

During the initial moments of a greeting, avoid:

- Giving him to-do's
- Expressing the frustrations of your day
- Treating him like a co-worker that has arrived to relieve you from your shift
- Being critical of something he did or didn't do

What you initially express sets the mood for the rest of the evening. If you've had a frustrating day and want to unload some of your grievances of the day, hold off sharing these while you are greeting one another. You can make time to share once he has settled in. It benefits you both to keep the disappointments of your day separate from your greeting.

Here is the danger in venting before you take that moment to connect and let him see your affection for him: if you start to dump all your frustrations of the day just when he arrives, he may misinterpret your venting as an indication of you being in a bad mood. Then, rather than connecting, he may disconnect to stay out of the line of fire or disengage to avoid saying anything that he feels will make matters worse.

In addition, he may interpret your frustration as you being upset with him. *Angry at the situation* can easily be misconstrued as *angry with him*. Do your best to postpone the venting session until a little later. Then, if you truly need to let off a little steam, state it briefly and include something sweet regarding him. Doing so will remove any confusion, and he will know that you are upset with the situation and not mad at him.

Here are some ways to vent your frustration in moderation while being clear that you're not angry with him:

> I almost lost it with the kids today, but I'm so delighted to see you that I'll put the weapons away.

> My boss nearly pushed me over the edge today. Knowing I was going to see you tonight kept me from falling apart.

> Today was pure chaos and I didn't get anything done, but I already feel better just seeing your face.

Try Your Best to Not Let Life Get In the Way

Life will get in the way of making this a regular routine if you let it. Two working adults with different schedules, having babies, long commutes, stressful jobs, multiple kids with extracurricular activities, working full time while completing a graduate program, you name it, life can get chaotic. It will take effort to keep a reunion ritual alive. Do your best not to let it fade into the background if you've missed a day or two. Instead, intentionally resurrect it so you can continue to create positive associations when you greet him, and you both look forward to the reunion.

Don't expect to achieve perfection with all your greetings. Some days life will throw you a curveball, and you'll be knee-deep in chaos. It's not about being perfect when you greet him; it's about taking the time to show him how much he matters to you. Even in the midst of chaos, you can spare 60 seconds to express your affection. If you can't greet him at the door with a warm embrace or a kiss because you are changing a diaper or on an important business call, you can still glance up and light up your face.

When you keep this ritual alive, you can better resist falling into the trap of taking him for granted.[35] Instead, it prompts you daily to nurture the positive side of your relationship. Greeting him well on a consistent basis has the power to transform your relationship. He will look forward to coming home because he knows you are waiting for him and, more importantly, that you are excited to see him. If you are the one coming home later than him, you can easily adapt these suggestions to match your needs. When you get home, simply take a moment to express your genuine happiness to see him.

Consider Creating One or More Connection Rituals

Like most couples, you were probably more intentional when you were falling in love about planning dates, having deep talks to better understand one another, and making time for each other. It was easier during that phase of the relationship, but now it requires that you purposely initiate moments of connection and intimacy.

One of the most effective methods to consciously strengthen a relationship is implementing connection rituals that make the moments you share together more purposeful and connected, even when you're extremely busy. A connection ritual is recurring, scheduled, and something you both feel is meaningful. According to research, couples who engage in rituals together are closer, more connected, have satisfaction in their relationship, and handle change better.[38]

The value of a connection ritual has less to do with the activity than what it signifies – that you are prioritizing one another and spending meaningful time together.[39] Regardless of what activity you select, it will strengthen your emotional intimacy when you deliberately maintain the practice because you both feel chosen and cherished.

Here is a list of various activities you can select from:

- Start a Sunday night ritual where you make sundaes together
- Take a dance class together – you can try ballroom dancing, swing dancing, salsa or even the tango if you want to add a little drama and flair
- Eat breakfast by candlelight
- Plan a weekly card night with just the two of you
- Volunteer for an organization you are both passionate about
- Pick a time daily (e.g., meal time) or weekly (e.g., Saturday night) where you agree to no electronics – no cell phones, computers, laptops, tablets, TV, gaming consoles, smartwatches, or other smart devices
- Start a chess tournament
- Take a shower together in the morning for a chance to connect before the day's hustle pulls you in different directions
- Redecorate a room or multiple rooms – the collaboration allows you both to channel your creative energies in the same direction
- Take a regular yoga class together
- Start a daily expression of gratitude ritual where you each give thanks for the big and small things done by the other person that day

- Start a New Year's journal together. In the first couple weeks of the new year, write down all the accomplishments and challenges from the previous year
- Garden together
- Each night, share your "high" and "low" moment of the day
- Build a pillow fort together
- Share a cup of tea or hot cocoa together while taking turns reading to one another
- Kick off or conclude your day with a walk around your neighborhood (or do it once or twice a week if you have limited time)
- Learn a new language together, and then plan a vacation where you can practice what you've learned. Or, if money is tight, plan to dine at an appropriate eatery that serves food from the region that speaks your newly acquired language
- Attend a weekly Taco Tuesday night at your favorite Mexican place or switch it up and try tacos at different locations every Tuesday
- Have a weekly night of playing boards games together
- Hold hands as you fall asleep

- Start a morning coffee chat ritual or an evening beverage coupled with a nightly talk
- Go through old pictures and talk about all the memories associated with each one
- Do crossword puzzles, Sudoku puzzles, or Wordle together
- Begin to keep an Anniversary diary where you two spend time each anniversary recording how you celebrated the day and include any highlights that occurred during the year (births, deaths, promotions, moves, etc.)
- Cook together
- Pick a time that has significance to you, like the time you got married, or 1:11, 2:22, 11:11, etc. Then, whoever sees that time first, says "Have I told you how much I love you today?"
- Have a weekly dominoes tournament
- Find a space where it won't be disturbed and start a jigsaw puzzle together
- Take indoor climbing lessons together – it will teach you trust and responsibility
- Sometimes it's too exhausting to go out on date night – instead, order in and then take a bath together and light candles
- Play tennis together weekly

- Start a happy dance ritual – it could be in the morning to set the mood for the day, when you two first see each other at the end of the day to celebrate being together again, saved for special moments of celebration, or anything that strikes your fancy
- Golf together – it will teach you patience
- Set up a private email address that only you two know – send each other random emails that are funny, cute and full of love
- Go for a run together – or if one of you runs too fast, the other can ride a bike alongside
- Start a Saturday morning ritual where you go to a coffee shop and read for an hour – even though you are reading in silence for that hour, the ritual includes the trip there, your particular coffee shop, the smells, the stillness, the return journey, all of which creates a special bond
- Join a co-ed softball team
- Set aside a regular time to pray or meditate together
- Take up canoeing – it's the perfect combination of being outside, being active, and being romantic
- Learn a new instrument together

- Follow a podcast that you are mutually interested in – it can lead to stimulating conversation
- Go on regular bike rides together
- Go birdwatching – it will cause you both to slow down and listen
- Have a weekly pizza night – at your favorite pizza place or get it delivered at home
- Going camping together can strengthen your romantic bonds while spending time in nature
- You may have different exercise routines, but you can coordinate and drive to/from the gym together
- Start a collection together, for example:
    - Stamps (together you can choose your area of interest and how you want to arrange your collection – then your search for stamps will be endless)
    - Coins (you can join a coin club together or visit local coin shows and coin shops)
    - Seashells (gets you taking long strolls along the seashore)
    - Vinyl records (involves trips to local vinyl shops or checking out estate sales)
    - Wine (a good excuse to go wine tasting regularly)

Picking any of these activities and doing them on a regular basis together will strengthen your relationship and draw you closer. Whether you call them rituals, traditions, or weekly practices, it doesn't matter what you label them. However, it is mandatory that you experience them together and that they develop into something you both look forward to. These shared experiences will create a special bond and provide you an opportunity to deepen the trust and intimacy in your relationship.

Mistake #9 – Top Takeaway Tips

♥ Offer meaningful greetings daily

♥ Look up and "light up" when you see him

♥ Carve out time for a regular shared activity

PAY IT FORWARD

If you found the information in this book helpful, I'd like to ask you a question before you move on to the final chapter.

Would you be willing to help another woman you've never met if it would only take a minute or two of your time and it didn't cost you anything?

If you answered yes, here's how you can help that unknown woman right now. She may be looking for information on how to improve communication in her relationship and could benefit from the material in this book.

As she's looking for a book, she'll be lured in by the title, but what convinces her to buy it will be the reviews. The more favorable reviews a book receives, the more inclined she will be to purchase it.

If you could take a minute to leave a review and share what you found valuable or any insights you've gained, your words may reassure her that this book contains useful tips and strategies to help her feel heard and understood in her relationship.

On the following page, you'll find two quick ways to be taken to the Amazon review page.

To leave a review,
just scan this QR code with your phone

Or visit TherapyBySue.com/reviewbook

Thank you for taking the time
to make a difference in another woman's life

FINAL WORDS

Now that you reached the end of the book, hopefully you've been inspired to approach conversations in your relationship in a new way. Instead of getting lost in the subject matter of your arguments, you now have the tools to take a step back from any miscommunication to observe whether the real problem lies in how you two approach communication differently.

You read some real-life examples of how something as simple as changing your phrasing can profoundly affect the reaction you get from your partner. We also discussed how the male mind often differs from yours in the way it operates when communicating and processing information. I hope this knowledge sparks new conversations with your partner as you seek to understand him as a unique individual. In turn, I hope he is open to learning about your uniqueness.

If you can see where things may have gone wrong – whether due to a false assumption, incorrect interpretation, or unsolicited advice – and you feel empowered to try to create a more open environment for communication, then you are on the right path. Furthermore, if you continue in this direction, it will lead to greater trust and respect for one another.

Take time now to identify which mistakes discussed in this book are problematic to your relationship and avoid making those. Ignore the rest if they don't apply. Be patient with yourself, and don't anticipate that you will stop making mistakes overnight. For example, say you forget and offer unsolicited advice. You have the option of apologizing at that moment or committing yourself to do better in the future. It will take time and practice with deliberate intent to break the old patterns. However, take to heart that each small, significant change you make will positively impact your relationship.

If there is one truth for you to hold onto, remember: *he is not you*. Accepting that your differences are normal and that there is no *right* way will help you remove the judgment and remain more loving. When you can, give him the benefit of the doubt. When you can't, make sure to ask questions first instead of assuming the worst.

With the insights you have gained from reading this book, you have discovered new ways to talk to him that don't inadvertently put him on the defense. Communicating more effectively will remove the barriers, and you will naturally feel more connected in your relationship. With trust and closeness restored, you will be in the best possible position to be heard and understood.

About the Author

Sue Shepard is a Licensed Marriage and Family Therapist and the author of *How to Talk to a Man and Feel Heard: 9 Mistakes Women Need to Avoid*.

Sue has been working with both couples and individuals for over 20 years and is passionate about helping people improve their relationships. Her first book focuses on communication issues, aiming to guide women towards better understanding in their relationships, and giving them the tools they need to not only communicate effectively with their partners, but also to feel confident that they're truly being heard.

Driving her writing is the culmination of years of experience and witnessing the relationship transformations triggered by simple changes. Sue sees the same communication issues arising for couples time and time again, and she knows that they can often be avoided by side-stepping common mistakes. Through her writing, she hopes to positively impact as many relationships as possible.

Sue has a four-legged assistant: her beloved rescue dog, Izzi, who clients claim has a deeply calming effect on them. In her spare time, Sue loves walking with Izzi on the beach, where she delights in collecting heart-shaped rocks. She also has a strong creative streak and finds joy in doing Alphabet Photography, blending this skill with design to create beautiful greetings cards.

Sue is devoted to work as a therapist and transitioned from a business career at IBM over two decades ago. She has a postgraduate degree in Clinical Psychology and currently sees clients in her private practice located in Orange County, California. Having personally benefited from therapy, Sue is of the firm belief that psychotherapy is a powerful tool for human growth, healing, and self-acceptance.

References

1. Gray J. *Men, Women and Relationships: Making Peace with the Opposite Sex.* 2nd ed. (Livingston J, ed.). Beyond Words Publishing; 1993.
2. Tannen D. *That's Not What I Meant! How Conversational Style Makes or Breaks Your Relationships.* Ballantine Books; 1992.
3. Hendrix H. *Keeping the Love You Find: A Personal Guide.* Simon & Schuster; 2003.
4. Rodgers S. The Silence of Men – How do Men Communicate in Relationships. Rodgerscounseling.com. Published March 3, 2016. Accessed November 20, 2021. http://rodgerscounseling.com/silence-men-men-communicate-relationships/
5. Tannen D. *You Just Don't Understand: Women and Men in Conversation.* Ballantine Books; 1991.
6. Gottman J, Silver N. *Why Marriages Succeed or Fail: And How You Can Make Yours Last.* Simon & Schuster; 1994.
7. Lusinski N. 9 Differences Between Accepting & Tolerating your Partner. Bustle.com. Published August 9, 2018. Accessed November 21, 2021. https://www.bustle.com/p/9-differences-between-accepting-tolerating-your-partner-10058335
8. McCarthy B, McCarthy EJ. *Getting It Right the First Time: Creating a Healthy Marriage.* Routledge; 2004.
9. Feldhahn S. *For Women Only: What You Need to Know about the Inner Lives of Men.* Revised and Updated Edition. Multnomah Press; 2013.

10. Feldhahn S. This is What Makes Your Man Vulnerable—Be Aware and Take Care! Shaunti.com. Published November 17, 2020. Accessed October 2, 2021. https://shaunti.com/2020/11/this-is-what-makes-your-man-vulnerable-be-aware-and-take-care/

11. Warner S. Develop Easy and Effective Communications with Him: How to Talk or Not Talk to a Man. Ezinearticles.com. Published September 8, 2012. Accessed October 2, 2021. https://ezinearticles.com/?Develop-Easy-and-Effective-Communications-With-Him:-How-To-Talk-Or-Not-Talk-To-A-Man&id=7265395

12. Schamuhn M. Is Your Unsolicited Advice Actually Helping Your Relationships? Margiecoach.com. Accessed September 25, 2021. https://www.margiecoach.com/is-your-unsolicited-advice-actually-helping-your-relationships/

13. Cullen K. Why No One Wants Unsolicited Advice (and What Actually Helps). Tinybuddha.com. Published December 26, 2017. Accessed September 25, 2021. https://tinybuddha.com/blog/no-one-wants-unsolicited-advice-actually-helps/

14. Martin S. It's Time to Stop Giving Unsolicited Advice. Psychcentral.com. Published February 27, 2020. Accessed September 25, 2021. https://psychcentral.com/blog/imperfect/2020/02/its-time-to-stop-giving-unsolicited-advice

15. Trent J. How to Create Emotional Word Pictures. FocusOnTheFamily.com. Published January 10, 2018. Accessed April 4, 2021. https://www.focusonthefamily.com/marriage/how-to-create-emotional-word-pictures/

16. Trent J. Bonus Chapter: 101 Life-Tested Word Pictures. Encouragingwords.com. Accessed July 31, 2021. https://encouragingwords.com/product/bonus-chapter-101-life-tested-word-pictures/

17. Lee S. The Dangerous Trap of Assumptions. CouplesInstituteCounseling.com. Accessed September 13, 2021. https://couplesinstitutecounseling.com/the-dangerous-trap-of-assumptions/

18. Stone D, Patton B, Heen S. *Difficult Conversations: How to Discuss What Matters Most*. Penguin; 1999.

19. Tannen D. Gender-specific Language Rituals. YouTube. Published December 27, 2013. https://www.youtube.com/watch?v=tUxnBZxsfoU

20. Damon C. Why You Should Never Ever, Ever Compare Your Husband to Another Man. Chelseadamon.com. Published July 6, 2016. Accessed October 9, 2021. http://chelseadamon.com/never-ever-compare-husband-another-man/

21. Lerner H. *Marriage Rules: A Manual for the Married and the Coupled Up*. Gotham Books; 2012.

22. Decker B. Eye Contact, Eye Communication and Eye Roll. Decker.com. Published October 26, 2009. Accessed September 11, 2021. https://decker.com/blog/eye-contact-eye-communication-and-eye-roll/

23. Brown D. How Eye Contact and Attraction are Linked. Regain.us. Updated July 28, 2021. Accessed September 11, 2021. https://www.regain.us/advice/attraction/how-eye-contact-and-attraction-are-linked/

24. Fullwood C, Doherty-Sneddon G. Effect of Gazing at the Camera During a Video Link on Recall. Appl Ergon. 2006; 37(2):167-175 https://www.sciencedirect.com/science/article/abs/pii/S000368700500089X?via%3Dihub

25. Gray J. *Men, Women and Relationships: Making Peace with the Opposite Sex*. 2nd ed. (Livingston J, ed.). Beyond Words Publishing; 1993.

26. Feldhahn S. Mystery Solved: 3 Things You Never Understood about How Your Wife Thinks. Shaunti.com. Published January 31, 2020. Accessed June 1, 2021. https://shaunti.com/2020/01/mystery-solved-3-things-you-never-understood-about-how-your-wife-thinks/

27. Ballew J. Make An Argument Worse in Two Words. Bodymindsoul.org. Published August 26, 2013. Accessed September 19, 2021. https://bodymindsoul.org/2013/08/make-an-argument-worse-in-two-words/

28. Hawkins AJ, Allen SE. How Many Married People Have Thought About Divorce? Ifstudies.org. Published November 2, 2015. Accessed September 18, 2021. https://ifstudies.org/blog/how-many-married-people-have-thought-about-divorce

29. Daniel-Farrell J. The Damaging Effect of Threatening a Divorce. Lifeconnectionscounseling.com. Published August 30, 2017. Accessed September 18, 2021. https://lifeconnectionscounseling.com/damaging-effect-threatening-divorce/

30. Borresen K. 7 Phrases You Should Never Say During an Argument. HuffPost. Published March 30, 2018. Accessed September 18, 2021. https://www.huffpost.com/entry/phrases-not-say-during-argument_n_5aba7beee4b03e2a5c76d26c

31. Joyce C. The Impact of Direct and Indirect Communication. Uiowa.edu. Published November 2012. Accessed October 10, 2021. https://conflictmanagement.org.uiowa.edu/sites/conflictmanagement.org.uiowa.edu/files/2020-01/Direct%20and%20Indirect%20Communication.pdf

32. Waterman A. How to Talk to a Man. Ezinearticles.com. Published January 11, 2007. Accessed October 11, 2021. https://ezinearticles.com/?How-to-Talk-to-a-Man&id=415497

33. Wingenbach TSH, Ashwin C, Brosnan M. Sex differences in facial emotion recognition across varying expression intensity

levels from videos. PLoS ONE. 2018;13(1):e0190634 10.1371/journal.pone.0190634

34. Tessina T. Asking for What You Want. Tinatessina.com. Accessed October 11, 2021. https://www.tinatessina.com/asking.html

35. McFadden P. 3 Daily Rituals That Stop Spouses From Taking Each Other for Granted. Gottman.com. Published October 11, 2017. Accessed October 21, 2021. https://www.gottman.com/blog/3-daily-rituals-that-stop-spouses-from-taking-each-other-for-granted/

36. Gonzales-Balado, JL. *Mother Teresa: In My Own Words*. Liguori Publications; 1997.

37. Becca. The BEST Marriage Tip. Thedatingdivas.com. Published November 5, 2015. Updated July 23, 2021. Accessed October 21, 2021. https://www.thedatingdivas.com/best-marriage-tip/

38. Brown HH. Examining The Relationship Between Connection Rituals and Marital Satisfaction: A Correlational Study. All Graduate Theses and Dissertations. USU.edu. 2839. Published May, 2007. Accessed October 21, 2021. https://digitalcommons.usu.edu/cgi/viewcontent.cgi?article=3846&context=etd

39. Stockhausen R, Milton J. The Ultimate 14 Step Guide to Build Emotional Intimacy in 2021. Practicalintimacy.com. Published April 7, 2021. Accessed October 21, 2021. https://practicalintimacy.com/how-to-build-emotional-intimacy-relationship/

40. Feldhahn S. The Two Words Your Husband Really Needs to Hear: Thank You. Shaunti.com. Published March 26, 2019. Accessed October 4, 2021. https://shaunti.com/2019/03/the-two-words-your-husband-really-needs-to-hear-thank-you/

Printed in Great Britain
by Amazon